Crystals for
Holistic Wellbeing

Practical Crystals

By Kathy Banegas
(@thehealinggem)

Illustrated by
Viki Lester
(@forensicsandflowers)

Contents

Chapter 5 : Crystals for Special Occasions 102

Chapter 6 : Crystals for Careers 120

Chapter 7 : Practical Crystal Grids 130

Black Moonstone

Celestite

Introduction

One day as I was driving home, I had a thought. Should I crash my car into the center divider and just end it all? I felt so hopeless and sad, like I just didn't want to go on. Then the beautiful faces of my three kids popped into my mind, and images of my husband and our wedding. Slowly, it was like I finally stopped holding my breath. I began to wake up and snap out of that horrible idea. I knew something had to change. There had to be a way I could feel like myself again. Three months earlier, I had lost my mother to breast cancer. I had taken on most of the responsibility of her care and funeral planning, and hadn't given myself the chance to grieve or even process the emotions. I was keeping it together for the image of keeping it together.

That night, I searched online for "holistic ways of healing," and as I scrolled through, I saw a shiny, purple spiky rock that called my attention. I clicked on the link and read all about the magical powers of Amethyst. I was intrigued, but also skeptical. About a week later as I drove home, I had a magical moment. A ray of sunlight hit a big store window, highlighting what seemed like Crystals! I pulled over and stepped inside this store where Clear Crystal points called to me. I bought one, which I still have today, placed it in my living room, and forgot about it for several days.

When I finally remembered about my new shiny rock, I realized I'd had the best few days in a long time. I was convinced it was the energy of this Crystal, and that day, I began my quest to learn all about them. Soon after, I was recommending Crystals for my family and friends to use in their own lives. My life changed because of these magical allies, Crystals.

Six years later in 2020, the world was faced with COVID-19. The uncertainty during this time caused a lot of fear and division when it came to treatment. Many people turned to Crystals, and I saw how people craved to work on themselves, to learn more about what was out there, and to find practical ways to integrate them into their already stressful lives.

This book is all about how you can incorporate the energy of Crystals in your day-to-day life in the most practical and easiest of ways. Some days you'll even forget they are there, but you'll definitely notice when they are not. I hope you enjoy this book and find that Crystals can do for you what they have done for me.

The following pages provide some easy ways to begin your own practical Crystal collection.

Choosing Your Crystals

Using Your Intuition

The most important thing when working with Crystals is that you follow what feels right to you. You know that feeling you get in the pit of your stomach when something isn't right or when something is exciting? That feeling is your intuition, your inner guidance, or your inner compass. You should always listen to your intuition. It is there to direct you, guide you, and protect you in every situation. Going against this feeling often makes you feel uncomfortable and yet we have all pushed it aside at times only to realize later we should have listened to ourselves. When it comes to Crystals and life in general, you should always listen to that inner voice. If you enter a metaphysical store looking for Crystals for relaxation but are quickly distracted by a shiny Crystal that is for focus, always go for the Crystal that calls you. Remember that your intuition knows what's best for YOU.

Using Your Senses

You can choose your Crystals by using your senses. How does it feel to the touch? Some people are not comfortable with certain textures. Close your eyes and hover the palms of your hands over the Crystals. Sometimes you can feel a tingle in the palms of your hands, or a change in temperature. Feeling nothing can also be an indication whether or not you should choose a certain Crystal for your collection.

You can also choose Crystals by the way they look. Perhaps you follow a certain aesthetic, or you pick your Crystals because they are your favorite color. Put your Crystals up to your ears and close your eyes. There might not be a sound, but you will be surprised by what you hear.

Caution: *I would not recommend using taste because some Crystals can be toxic, or contain dirt that should not be ingested.*

Using a Pendulum

Pendulums are directed by our own higher self's knowing and this can be a good way to decide on a Crystal that you are not sure about for your collection. If you are unfamiliar with pendulums, here is a quick and easy way to use one:

1. Pick a pendulum you connect with. It can be made of Crystal or any material that calls you.

2. Spend a little time putting your energy into it. You can do this by carrying the pendulum with you for a day or even placing it under your pillow for a night.

3. Once you have connected with it, hold the chain with your dominant hand (the hand you write with) and place your non-dominant hand under it.

4. Ask the pendulum to show you "YES." The pendulum should begin to move back-and-forth or in a circular motion. This movement will mean "YES.

5. Ask the pendulum to show you "NO." The pendulum should then move in the opposite motion.

6. Once you have your responses you can begin to ask it questions, such as: "Is this Crystal right for me?" or: "Should I purchase this Crystal to add to my collection?"

Doing Research

One of the best ways to begin your Crystal collection is to research their properties. This book is the perfect tool for finding the Crystals you need by their energetic properties. If you are trying to attract abundance you can look for Crystals that are known for helping people attract this in particular. You can also do your own personal research by working with Crystals directly and seeing which ones work for you and which don't. Once you are a seasoned collector you will have a group of Crystals that you go to for certain things.

As you read this book you might notice that some of the "Crystals" mentioned are not actually Crystals. For example, Ammonite is actually a fossil. However, all have energetic healing properties that can help you through your life journey, and this is why I have included them under the term "Crystals."

Amber

Fluorite

Ruby

Cleansing Your Crystals

Once you have selected your Crystals you might ask: "What do I do next?" The next step to using your Crystal collection is cleansing them, as you want to eliminate any energy they might have collected on their journey. Crystals can absorb negative energy from their environment so if your Crystal was held by someone who wasn't having a good day, it may have kept some of that energy.

It is important to cleanse your Crystals before using them, and also cleanse them periodically so that they continue to work at their fullest potential. In the same way as if you don't cleanse the lint trap or filter of a clothes dryer, the debris will continue to accumulate and the dryer won't dry as fast; if you don't give your Crystals a regular, energetic cleanse, their energy can dull.

Here are some practical ways to cleanse your Crystals.

With Your Intention

As humans, we are so powerful that we can direct energy with just our intention. If you wake up in the morning and set your intention to have a positive outlook, you will most likely have a positive day. Similarly, you can set an intention for your Crystals to be cleansed of all the energy they have absorbed. You can do this by following this simple practice.

1. Choose the Crystal you want to cleanse.

2. Hold it between your palms without letting your fingers touch.

3. Lift your Crystal to eye level. Softly gaze at your Crystal and send it the intention that you want it to be cleansed of all the energy it has absorbed. You can even picture that your Crystal looks squeaky clean. Gaze at your Crystal for as long as you want and when you feel it's ready you can relax your eyesight and set your Crystal down. It is now clean and ready to work with.

Under Running Water

One of the easiest ways to cleanse your Crystals is to place them under running water. Simply turn on your water and give your Crystals a good, thorough rinse.

Please note that not all Crystals are safe for water. If you decide to rinse your Crystals under water, make sure they are safe to be wet. Here are the Crystals in this book that are best kept away from water cleansing: Agatized Coral, Amazonite, Amber, Angelite, Apatite (Blue and Green), Aquamarine, Calcite (all types), Celestite, Chrysocolla, Copper, Desert Rose, Fluorite, Golden Topaz, Hematite, Jasper (all types), Kunzite, Kyanite (all types), Labradorite, Lapis Lazuli, Lepidolite, Malachite, Moonstone (all types), Pyrite, Ruby (all types), Selenite, Tangerine Quartz, Turquoise, and Ulexite.

With Ocean Waves

Energetically cleanse your Crystals by letting the ocean water wash over them. Salt is a great cleanser and, together with the ocean waves, this makes for a powerful way to cleanse your Crystals. There are two things to consider with this process. First, only water-safe Crystals can be cleansed this way. Second, you have to hold your Crystals carefully so that strong waves don't wash them away. I personally put my Crystals in a mesh drawstring bag. This allows me to hold the bag by the handle, so I won't lose my Crystals as they are being cleansed by the water.

With Smoke

Smoke cleansing is my favorite way to cleanse my Crystals because it's easy and efficient. All you need for this process is incense or dried herbs and your intention. You can use any incense that releases smoke such as incense sticks or resins that are burned with charcoal. You can use dried herbs that you have cut from your garden or herb bundles, such as Sage, Yerba Santa, or Rosemary, which can be found at any metaphysical store. Once you have lit your incense or herb, hold your Crystal directly over the smoke or bring the smoke toward your Crystals. The purpose is to have the smoke surround the entire Crystal. As you watch the smoke enveloping your Crystals, set the intention that this smoke is to cleanse your Crystals.

By Burying in Soil

There are only a few ways to cleanse your Crystals and charge them at the same time (read about what it means to charge your Crystals on page 11), and burying them in soil is one of them. Bury your Crystals in a potted plant, or in your yard or garden,

ensuring they are fully covered by the soil. Once buried, leave them for at least six hours, or preferably for an entire day. Remember to leave a marker indicating their location to find them again.

Under the Sun

Placing your Crystals outside in the Sun or on a sunny windowsill for one to two hours is another way you can both cleanse and charge them. Be aware though that if left under the Sun for too long, some Crystals (those vibrant in color such as Rose Quartz and Amethyst) will lose their color.

With Sound

Energetically cleanse your Crystals by giving them a sound bath using any type of sound, such as a singing bowl, a rattle, or even your voice. Set your Crystals down and hum a tune or pretend you are the star of the opera. Set your intention and visualize the sound waves breaking them free of their stuck energy. Remember, you don't have to be musically talented to use this process of cleansing.

Rice, Salt, or Flowers

Cleanse your Crystals by placing them in a bowl of white or brown rice, sea salt, or flower petals. Fill a bowl with one of these items and submerge your Crystal in it. Leave it for a few hours, then remove your Crystal when you feel it is ready. You can reuse this bowl and its ingredients a few more times to cleanse other Crystals, but do not reuse the rice, salt, or flowers for cooking. The ingredients will have absorbed the energy that was in your Crystals, so it's best to throw them away.

Programming Your Crystals

Now that you have cleansed your Crystals it's time to decide which ones you want to program. Programming your Crystals means that you have a job for them to do and you want to make sure they know what that job is. This is important because you want the Crystal you are programming to focus all of its energy into helping you achieve or accomplish the job you give it. For example, you can program Lapis Lazuli to help you boost your confidence, Citrine to help you attract more abundance, and Clear Quartz, known as "The Master Healer," to do virtually anything.

Remember, you don't have to program every Crystal if you don't want to. Crystals will still bring healing energy into your space even when they are not programmed.

Setting Clear Intentions

Before starting the process of programming your Crystals, it is important to have a clear intention in mind for each Crystal. Take a little time for self-reflection. What are some things you want to improve in your life right now? What are some goals that you would like to accomplish and achieve?

If you would like to find a new career, your intention may be: "I wish to attract new career opportunities and have the courage to follow and pursue these opportunities." If you are looking to find love, it may be: "I invite love and when love comes to me, I am open and accepting." Or, if you are looking to attract money, instead of saying: "I want to be a millionaire," say something like: "I will receive the financial opportunities I need and I will be successful at everything I put my mind and energy into."

Lapis Lazuli

Citrine

How to Program Your Crystals

Here are a few easy steps to program your Crystals:

1. Choose the Crystal you will be programming.

2. Choose a quiet and peaceful location that will allow you to connect with your Crystal. Make this a sacred space by lighting incense or a candle and playing relaxing music.

3. Hold your Crystal between your palms, without your fingers touching. Raise your hands to eye level so you can gaze at it, or hold your Crystal at your heart center by placing it over the center of your chest, with both hands over the Crystal.

4. Tell your Crystal your intention. Repeat this intention into your Crystal, in your mind or out loud. Repeat it until you feel the Crystal's energy and your intention's energy have connected.

5. You can now work with your Crystal. Carry it with you or put it in a space you spend the most time in. If you programmed a piece of Crystal jewelry, you can now wear it.

Red Jasper

Clear Quartz

Rose Quartz

Amethyst

Charging Your Crystals

It's important to charge your Crystals. Just like a battery needs recharging to work at its fullest potential, a Crystal needs charging to help you achieve and accomplish your intentions. If you sense that your Crystal's energy is feeling dull, tired, or your intentions are not coming to fruition, it's time to give them a little charge.

Under a Full Moon

Charge your Crystals under the Full Moon once a month by leaving them outside overnight. If you can only leave them out for a few hours or minutes, that's ok. You can also put them on a windowsill overnight where the moonlight will still hit them. Even if you can't see the Moon, it is still shining through the night's sky.

Many believe that not all Full Moons are safe for Crystal charging. For example, it is not recommended to charge Crystals during any Lunar or Solar eclipses. Eclipse energy can be intense, chaotic, and unpredictable and you do not want to charge your Crystals with this energy. Instead, wait until the next Full Moon and, during eclipses, focus on grounding and cleansing Crystals that you haven't cleansed in a while. Some Full Moons may also seem too intense for you, in which case, sit that Full Moon out and refrain from charging your Crystals. Use your intuition to guide you.

Burying in Soil

Burying your Crystals in the soil is one of the few ways to cleanse and charge your Crystals together. Bury your Crystals in your yard or garden, or even in a potted plant. Leave your Crystals fully submerged in soil for at least twenty-four hours for full benefits. Dig them up the next day, and you will have fully charged Crystals.

Under the Sun

Placing your Crystals outside in the Sun or on a sunny windowsill for one to two hours is another way you can both cleanse and charge them. Remember though that if left under the Sun for longer than the recommended time, some Crystals will lose their color.

With Clear Quartz

Clear Quartz, also known as "The Master Healer," can act as an amplifier to help you charge your Crystals. Simply place the Crystal you wish to charge on top of a large Clear Quartz cluster for about twenty-four hours. Smaller pieces of Clear Quartz will not give your Crystal the full recharge it needs.

Crystal Charging Pages

These are charging pages I have created for this book that you can charge your Crystals with at any time. Open your book to these pages and place it outside during a Full Moon. The pages will be charged with Full Moon energy, making it possible for you to then charge your Crystals at any time by placing your Crystals on these pages for at least six hours. Sometimes we miss the Full Moon and wish we could have charged our Crystals. This makes for a fun and simple solution! Periodically recharge these charging pages by setting them outside during any Full Moon.

Building a Practical Crystal Collection

Amethyst possesses the qualities of a BFF. It helps you feel calm and tranquil in times of stress, and to quit old habits so you don't keep making the same mistakes. If you have trouble sleeping Amethyst can calm your mind. Amethyst is purple, which means it helps balance your Crown Chakra, the center for spiritual growth, opening you up to learning new things and growing emotionally and spiritually. Place a piece of Amethyst under your pillow to help balance your Crown Chakra.

Clear Quartz can be programmed to help you heal, achieve, and overcome anything. It takes negative energy from your aura and surroundings and transforms it into positive energy. Its clarity in color brings you clarity of mind so that you can release anything that no longer serves your greatest purpose. Clear Quartz amplifies everything that is positive so that what is good can be great! Place a Clear Quartz with your other Crystals so that it can amplify all of their energies.

Rose Quartz is the Crystal of love and self-love. It encourages you to perform acts of love for yourself, and eliminates negative self-talk and limiting beliefs so that when you look in the mirror, you feel beautiful. It can help you love yourself again. Wear Rose Quartz daily to start being inspired to prioritize self-love.

Selenite is one of the few Crystals that does not require cleansing or charging because it does not absorb energy. Instead, it cleanses negative energy out of any space. It can also draw out and eliminate the energy absorbed by other Crystals. Place Crystal jewelry on top of Selenite slabs, bowls, or towers, and leave them overnight for freshly cleansed Crystal jewelry.

Black Tourmaline removes negative energy and protects you from it. If someone is sending you ill will and bad intentions, Black Tourmaline creates a shield so that it cannot affect you. It also balances your Root Chakra so that you feel rooted into the earth; stable, and protected. Place Black Tourmaline at your front door to act as a filter for anything and everyone coming in.

Citrine brings joy, energy, happiness, creativity, good luck, and more! Its energy balances your Solar Plexus Chakra, which is at the core of who you are. Citrine can reignite the fire within that you thought you had lost. Get ahold of your Citrine and reimagine all the dreams you thought were too big. Place Citrine anywhere you want its high vibration to bring you happiness, energy, and creativity. To bring abundance into your life, place a small piece of Citrine in your wallet.

Clear Quartz

Amethyst

Rose Quartz

These Crystals are great for a beginner's set, especially if you are limited in the number of Crystals you can get. I recommend starting your collection with a small piece of each of these. They can help you achieve anything your heart desires.

Citrine

Black Tourmaline

Selenite

Crystal Shapes

Crystals come in many different shapes, and these shapes themselves have energetic properties that can help your intentions come to life. To help you choose the perfect Crystal shape to work with, here is a list of some Crystal shape carvings included in this book and their energetic purpose:

Cluster

Crystal clusters are a family of points that grew together on the same matrix. They have an energetic superpower because they are connected and working together. They eliminate negative energy and amplify the positive energy of Crystals around them. Place clusters where people gather such as an office or living room to bring a sense of unity, cooperation, and peace.
Example: Smoky Quartz

Tumbled Stone

Tumbled stones are Crystals that were placed inside a machine called a tumbler, which spins and spins until the Crystals become smooth. They are a great way to start your Crystal collection as you can obtain many types of Crystals in a small form less expensively. They are versatile and easy to carry around with you and place in a variety of spaces.
Example: Moss Agate

Slab, Plates, and Bowls

Crystal slabs, plates, and bowls are neat and fun ways to display your jewelry, Crystals, and trinkets, and can also charge these items with the energy of the Crystal the piece is made of. Selenite is a particularly great Crystal for this purpose.
Example: Grossularite

Smoky Quartz   Moss Agate   Grossularite

Palm Stone

Palm stones are shaped in a smooth, rounded form to hold easily in the palm of your hand. They help you feel grounded, more centered, and give you something tangible to hold in times of stress, anxiety, and pressure. You can also meditate while holding palm stones or use them in a Crystal Healing or Reiki session. *Example:* Ruby in Kyanite

Points and Towers

Points and towers have much the same properties, but whereas a point is naturally formed in the earth, a tower is cut to have six or eight sides and a flat base for standing. Points and towers focus their energy in one specific direction and emit energy from their tip. This makes them great for manifesting rituals, Crystal grids (see Chapter 7), and healing sessions of different modalities. *Example:* Lemon Quartz

Sphere

Spheres are one of the hardest and time-consuming Crystal shapes to create as the carver has to make each side perfectly smooth. Their round shape emits harmony and energy in all directions and helps you overcome insecurities, fears, and self-sabotage. Crystal spheres are great tools for meditation, cleansing negative energy from any space, and even massage. *Example:* Rainbow Moonstone

Raw or Rough

Raw or rough Crystals are exactly as they were originally found. Their shapes are unusual, awkward, and some might even say unattractive. However, many collectors prefer raw Crystals because of their natural beauty, myself included. Since they are in their purest form, raw Crystals contain the purest of energies. They can bring you healing, awareness, and transformation. *Example:* Bloodstone

Ruby in Kyanite

Lemon Quartz

Rainbow Moonstone

Bloodstone

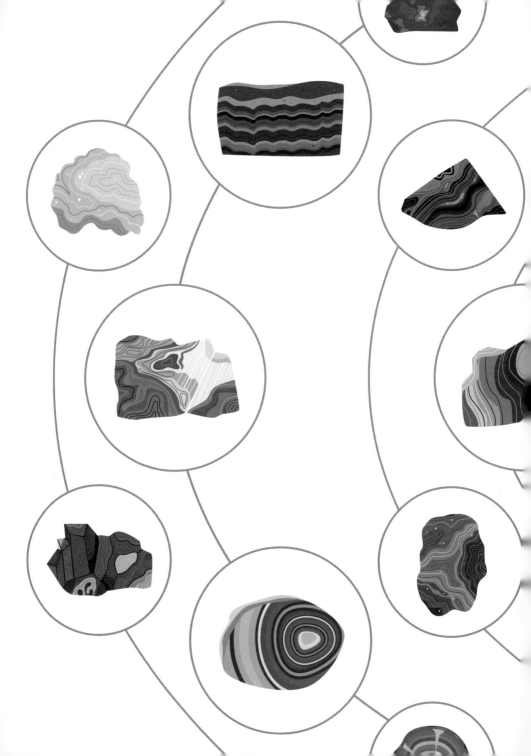

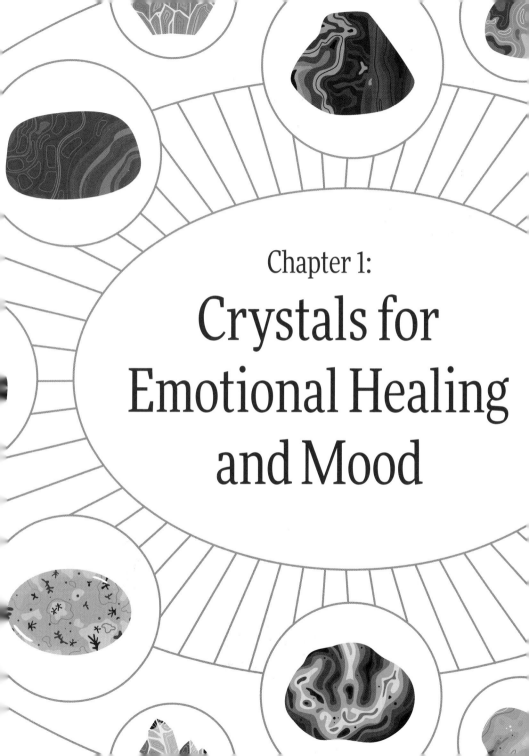

Chapter 1:
Crystals for Emotional Healing and Mood

Tiger's Eye

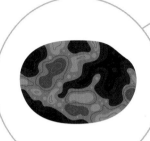

Rhodonite

Fluorite

Crystals for Confidence

Do you trust yourself? Having confidence means that you trust in your abilities and yourself. These Crystals for confidence can help you get to a place where you feel secure in yourself and what you have to offer.

Orange Calcite

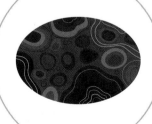

Ruby

Turquoise

Rhodonite brings self-acceptance by releasing emotional blockages. Once you can accept yourself, your confidence will soar! Bring your Rhodonite Crystal to any love-centered meetings, like a friend's hangout, or even on a first date.

Tiger's Eye is known for its ability to help you step into your power. It encourages you to push through and be seen in situations where you otherwise might try to hide or blend in. Wear it as a necklace the next time you have an important business meeting.

Fluorite is a stone of the mind that brings mental clarity by absorbing and eliminating any stress you might be feeling. When the stress is gone you will remember that you have nothing to worry about and that you can be confident. Put Fluorite in your pocket or in a little pouch and carry daily to elevate your vibration.

Turquoise helps you speak your truth with ease and from a place of love. This helps even the shyest person feel more confident in themselves. Place a Turquoise at the center of your throat and take a few deep breaths. This will help center you and feel more confident in what you need to say.

Ruby is ruled by the Sun, which is where it gets its vitalizing energy and mesmerizing color. When worn you can feel a surge of fresh energy as it ignites your fire, inner strength, and self-confidence. Wear Ruby in a piece of jewelry to feel spiritually and physically confident. Wear it when you want to stand out.

Orange Calcite brings out the joy in life and helps you forget all the cares and worries you had before you held it. It will boost your inner confidence by shining a light on any insecurities that are putting a damper on your day. Hold a small piece in your hand when old insecurities start creeping in.

Snakeskin Agate

Sunstone

Peridot

Crystals for Joy

There's nothing like that radiant feeling that fills you from head to toe when you feel joy, but sometimes daily stresses can dim that radiance. If you feel like your inner joy has been dimmed, work with the following Crystals.

Green Tourmaline

Alexandrite

Charoite

Snakeskin Agate reminds you that even when things get tough, things will always get better. It brings optimism in the hardest of times and energizes its wearer. Place it on your Solar Plexus Chakra for five minutes, to help elevate your mood and bring joy back into your life.

Sunstone is known for its sparkly metallic glitter, and inclusions of Hematite and Copper that are reminiscent of the Sun's rays. Just like the Sun's rays, Sunstone illuminates your path and purpose, restoring the joy in even the littlest things. Place your Sunstone in the Sun to charge for half an hour and then place at your desk to spark up feelings of joy.

Peridot has proven throughout history to bring its owners clarity of mind, personal growth, prosperity, and joy. Records indicate that Peridot was mined as early as 1500 BC and that Cleopatra's famous Emerald collection was actually Peridot. Carrying Peridot in your purse or pocket will ward off negativity, leaving space for joyous energy only.

Charoite is a Crystal of perspective, helping you discern what is for the highest good. It assists in releasing fears and anything that is blocking you from experiencing joy. Meditate with Charoite to help you see more clearly what could be hindering you from experiencing joy.

Alexandrite is known for its magical color-changing abilities. Sometimes appearing purplish-red or blue and green depending on the angle you are looking from, Alexandrite calls you to look at situations in your life from all possible angles. Even when you are feeling hopeless, you can find blessings and joy in this Crystal. Place a piece of Alexandrite in the center of your home to ensure it is always a joyful place.

Green Tourmaline encourages you to think for yourself, try new things, and not take anything too seriously. It also stimulates self-compassion so that you are not hard on yourself. When you are too hard on yourself, you block the joy that comes from the simplicity of life. Wear Green Tourmaline as a piece of jewelry that touches your heart so that it can bring emotional healing and joy.

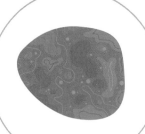

Sunstone

Dendritic Agate

Amazonite

Crystals for Productivity

I tend to leave certain tasks until the last minute. I procrastinate, then it's two hours later and I still haven't begun my task. If you can relate to this, the Crystals on this page may help you be more productive.

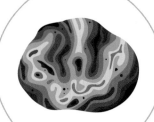

Copper

Howlite

Sodalite

Dendritic Agate looks like a picturesque forest and helps you stay grounded and connected to Mother Earth. Its grounding properties also help you stay level-headed and focused on the tasks ahead so that you can be productive. Carry Dendritic Agate along with other productivity energy Crystals to amplify the energy.

Sunstone is supercharged with energy to help you be productive. It uplifts your mood so that you feel ready to take on any to-do list or long-term project. It also has the power to cleanse and clear all your Chakras so that they are bright and squeaky clean, allowing the energy in your body to flow more freely. Wear Sunstone when you are out in the sunlight to magnify its energy.

Amazonite is a Crystal that can help you communicate clearly and effectively. If you have been assigned to complete a task and you need to delegate duties, this is the Crystal to work with. It's perfect for people in leadership roles, allowing you to deliver instructions clearly and calmly. Bring it along to any study groups or work meetings.

Sodalite is known as the "Thinker's Stone" because it can calm an overactive mind, eliminating any distractions that are preventing you from staying focused and being productive. When you start to lose focus on your tasks, close your eyes, hold a small Sodalite up to your Third Eye Chakra, and take a few deep breaths. The energy of Sodalite can reset your thoughts and you should be able to focus again.

Howlite has a calm and relaxed energy that allows you to approach any task with soothing clarity and calmness. Its soothing energy says: "I have your back. Slow and steady, slow and steady." Before you know it, you have been productive without knowing you were even working. Place Howlite on top of your desk, your books, or your projects before you start working on them and it will surround all your items with a sense of clarity and calm.

Copper stimulates the flow of energy in the body. It activates the Sacral Chakra, which is the center for energy in the body. It can combat any fatigue you are feeling that is preventing you from being productive. Since Copper is an energy conductor it's best to wear in jewelry so that it can keep your energy levels and productivity high!

Ruby in Kyanite

Ocean Jasper

Tangerine Quartz

Crystals for Positive Thinking

Are you a cup half-empty or a cup half-full kind of person? If you answered half-empty, chances are that you struggle with positive thinking. For more positive thoughts, check out the following Crystals.

Sugilite

Pyrite

Fluorite

Ruby in Kyanite is a power duo that can help you live your happiest life. Ruby can be used when you are feeling low and tired, since fatigue and sadness can bring negative thoughts. Kyanite is a Crystal of intuition and calming. Together the duo restores balance to bring back your positive mindset. Rub a Ruby in Kyanite worry stone when you are feeling nervous, anxious, or worried—it will bring in positivity to your auric field.

Ocean Jasper is one of those Crystals you look at and immediately feel warm and peaceful. Just like the ocean, it exudes calming, nurturing, and positive energy. It reminds you that no obstacle is too big to overcome and that you can let go of your worries. Wearing Ocean Jasper daily can really change your outlook on life so that you can remain positive even in the most challenging of situations.

Tangerine Quartz is created through a combination of Quartz and Hematite, bringing the positive, amplifying qualities of Clear Quartz, and the gentle grounding of Hematite together. It illuminates and brings awareness to your feelings and thoughts. Thinking positively will bring you calm, focus, and grounding, so if you are having negative thoughts that are bringing you down, hold a piece of Tangerine Quartz for five minutes to help change the direction of your thoughts.

Fluorite is the Crystal of mental order. It can help you declutter your mind so that you can welcome positive physical, mental, and spiritual energy into your life. Fluorite will also help you make space in your mind for clear thinking, purpose, and can even improve your memory. Set an intention with a Fluorite Crystal by holding it up to your Third Eye, between your eyebrows, and asking it to bring you positive thinking, the ability to retain information, and peace of mind.

Pyrite is a positive electrical charge for your brain. Just looking at Pyrite will bring happiness, liveliness, and positive thoughts. Pyrite also stimulates creativity and imagination. Add a small nugget of Pyrite to your Crystal pouch to keep emotions balanced and to remind yourself that you can overcome any obstacles. You just have to think positive!

Sugilite is a Crystal that helps you focus on positive solutions for any situation. It promotes forgiveness and self-love, eliminating negative and intrusive thoughts so they can be replaced with positive thoughts. Sugilite brings its wearer strength, hope, and positive energy. Wear it daily in a necklace or bracelet until you feel that positive thinking is coming more easily.

Mangano Calcite

Apache Tears

Rutilated Quartz

Crystals for Forgiveness

The act of forgiving is an intentional decision to let go of anger and resentment. It is important to forgive so that you can make space for positive things in your life. These Crystals can help you let go and make way for new blessings.

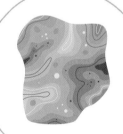

Chrysoprase

Rhodochrosite

Serpentine

Mangano Calcite is a stone of forgiveness that helps you release fear and grief. By releasing and choosing to let go of stuck energy you are opening yourself up for new blessings such as unconditional love. Place a piece of Mangano Calcite under your pillow the next time you are having trouble forgiving so that it can gently and slowly help you through the process.

Apache Tears, legend has it, are the tears shed by the families of Apache warriors who were lost in battle. As each family member shed their tears, the tears turned to stone before hitting the ground. If carried with you, an Apache Tears Crystal can help to alleviate the pain in grief and stop your tears since they have already been shed by others for you. It is easier to give or accept forgiveness once grief has passed. Meditate while holding this Crystal if forgiving has been hard for you to do lately.

Rutilated Quartz illuminates what has been swept under the rug. When you are holding on to grudges or ill feelings, you tend to hide them in your subconscious. Rutilated Quartz brings light to these situations so that you can face them, forgive, and let them go once and for all. Place Rutilated Quartz on a windowsill so that when the sunlight hits the Crystal it can radiate rays of light into parts of your life in which you need to practice forgiveness.

Serpentine is a powerful Crystal that draws out negative thoughts and feelings. It also helps clear the heart of hurtful and painful emotions. Once it has balanced, the heart allows you to feel compassion and give and receive forgiveness. If you are having a hard time forgiving and letting go, wear Serpentine over your heart.

Rhodochrosite is a Crystal of love that encourages forgiveness for others and for yourself. It helps you get to a point where you are willing to release and let go of hurt you are holding in your heart and mind. Rhodochrosite also helps you understand that forgiving doesn't mean it's ok, but that it is important to do for your own personal healing. If you are having difficulty finding the strength and energy to forgive, hold Rhodochrosite in your non-dominant hand (also known as your receiving hand) to receive its loving energy.

Chrysoprase is a calming Crystal that brings hope, compassion, and love. It also encourages the release of negative feelings so that you are able to forgive and drop any grudges that you might be holding on to. Use Chrysoprase in a Crystal grid for forgiveness (for more on grids see Chapter 7). Leave the grid in a safe and secure place for as long as is needed and until you feel that you have extended or received forgiveness.

Iolite

Snowflake Obsidian

Fluorite

Crystals for Focus

We live in a busy world of endless distractions. There always seems to be so many things, pulling in so many directions. If you want to focus more on what matters, then get to know the following Crystals.

Blue Sapphire

Hematite

Albite

Iolite is a Crystal for vision and ambition. It is perfect for staying focused on any project with a deadline since it will provide you with the clarity you need to make a plan of attack, and the ambition and motivation to get it done. Place Iolite in the immediate area where you will be working and completing your project.

Snowflake Obsidian is a purifier that removes negativity from any stressful or anxiety-inducing situation that makes it hard to focus. It will calm you and help you feel grounded so that you can get back to focusing on and completing any task at hand. In the Stone Age, Obsidian was used to make weapons such as arrowheads. Add a Snowflake Obsidian arrowhead to your Crystal collection to harness its focused and warrior-like energy.

Fluorite is possibly the most popular Crystal for focus. It is popular amongst students because of its ability to help you retain information, organize your thoughts, and stay focused in stressful environments. Fluorite helps support the mind, allowing you to keep sharp, hone in on your goals, and find success. Place a Fluorite Crystal at your desk or workspace and it will bring you much success while you study or tackle a complicated project.

Albite encourages you to follow your dreams by eliminating the fear of failure and boosting self-confidence. It helps you focus on making your dreams a reality even if it means facing challenges. Albite supports you through the growing pains of personal transformation. If you have been putting off your own needs and wants because you don't know where to begin, carry Albite with you and start focusing on bringing your best life into fruition.

Hematite is known for its protective qualities, but rarely given credit for its gentle grounding properties. It has the ability to gently relieve mental stress, which keeps you from thinking clearly and from being able to connect to your creative abilities. When you work with Hematite your mind can focus on tasks and projects so that you can finish what you started. The next time you need to complete a project and are struggling to focus, wear a Hematite bracelet on your receiving hand to take in its grounding and focused energy.

Blue Sapphire is a powerful Crystal that can help you achieve mastery over your mind. Too many negative thoughts can bring about brain fog and distraction, and negatively affect your actions and emotions. If you don't learn to distinguish healthy thoughts from negative ones, you can face many issues in life. Blue Sapphire can help stop thoughts that are not serving you and allow you to focus on those that will help you achieve the life you want to live.

Garnet

Pink Tourmaline

Malachite

Crystals for Love

There are many types of love that we can experience in our lives: friendship, family love, self-love, romantic love, and unconditional love. The following Crystals can help attract the type of love that you need most into your life.

Rhodochrosite

Unakite

Pink Opal

Garnet gets its name from the Latin word *garanatus*, meaning "seed-like," because of its resemblance to Pomegranate seeds. Pomegranate has symbolized femininity and fertility for many generations and in many cultures. Garnet brings fertility in love, passion, and romance. Gift it to your spouse on your second wedding anniversary, according to etiquette writer Emily Post's 1912 list of suggested wedding anniversary gems. This has since been endorsed by several gemology associations and been followed by happy couples for decades.

Pink Tourmaline brings a warm and secure feeling to your heart. It allows you to open up and feel safe giving and receiving love. It is the perfect Crystal for compassionate love, understanding love, and gentle love. If you are looking for love, set your intentions into a piece of Pink Tourmaline. Hold it to your heart center and tell it exactly what you want in your next romantic relationship.

Malachite is known for its anchoring energy since it helps you feel grounded and connected to the earth. Known for its heart healing and protective energy, Malachite's energy helps you see love in a clear and grounded way by balancing your Heart Chakra. It helps you heal any emotional wounds and traumas that are holding you back from finding the type of love that you need and deserve in your life. Gift a matching Malachite heart to a friend, lover, or family member to strengthen your bond.

Pink Opal promotes self-love and helps to heal deep emotional wounds. If you are looking to heal from a recent broken heart, Pink Opal is the right Crystal for you since it helps to ease anxiety and find forgiveness for yourself and for others. To work with Pink Opal, hold it with your receiving hand, close your eyes, and take deep breaths as you envision its soft pink light surrounding your heart.

Unakite is the perfect Crystal for love because it contains green and pink, the two colors associated with the Heart Chakra. It gently encourages you to release resentment and old emotional traumas you have been holding onto. It is a perfect Crystal for relationships because it aids in releasing toxic behaviors that may be affecting your connections. To bring Heart Chakra healing, place it under your pillow when you go to sleep and ask your Unakite to bring you heart balance as you rest.

Rhodochrosite helps bring your desires to fruition. If your wish is to find true love, Rhodochrosite can help you attract people that you have a genuine connection with. If you feel you have lost all hope in love, hold your Rhodochrosite and make a wish. It will bring you hope and help make all your love dreams come true.

Green Apatite

Gray Botswana Agate

Hiddenite

Crystals for Gratitude

When was the last time you took the time to really thank someone, and express gratitude for what a gesture meant to you? If you would like to grow in your feelings of gratitude, the Crystals on this page are for you.

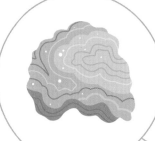

Stilbite

Lava Stone

Tree Agate

Green Apatite helps awaken your appetite for life. It helps you to be grateful for the little things and the big things and purifies negativity from your life so that you can see all of the positives. Since it is green it also helps to bring emotional balance and highlight the things that truly bring you joy and happiness. Bring a piece of Green Apatite when you go out, to help you see the beauty in everything and spark up feelings of gratitude for what you have.

Gray Botswana Agate is known for the comfort it brings people who are going through a difficult time. Named after the area in Africa where it is mined, it brings hope, comfort, and inner stability, and creates a sense of gratitude for life and the opportunity to keep going. Meditate with a piece of Gray Botswana Agate by staring at its "eye" formation, allowing it to send you its comforting and insightful energy.

Hiddenite supports personal growth and development. It highlights all of the blessings in your life so that you feel gratitude for everything you already have, and helps you find a genuine appreciation for all of the positivity that surrounds you so that you are more open to new possibilities and opportunities. Place your Hiddenite in a space where you spend the most time, so that you are always reminded of your blessings.

Tree Agate is a Crystal that helps you appreciate the beauty of nature and everything that Mother Earth does for its inhabitants. It teaches forgiveness, selflessness, and gratitude for our life-giving planet. It reminds that, just as our planet is always changing, so, too, you must change and grow. Spend a day in nature with Tree Agate, taking in its beauty. Let it fill you with gratitude for every tree, every plant, and every living thing.

Lava Stone is formed when lava cools, and can be found anywhere in the world where there is volcanic activity. It is not a Crystal, but belongs to the volcanic igneous rock family. This does not mean it lacks healing properties, though. Because of how it is formed, Lava Stone has a very grounding yet gentle energy that fills its owner with courage, peace, and gratitude. Wear Lava stone in jewelry that touches your skin directly, to raise your vibration and be filled with gratitude.

Stilbite brings the warmest of energies through its soft shades and warm colors. It brings gentle balance, calm, inner peace, clarity, and gratitude. It also helps open up you heart to universal love so that you may move forward and connect to spirit realms where you can ask for guidance. Meditate with Stilbite and envision yourself being enveloped by a soft pillowy energy filling your heart with peace and gratitude.

Ulexite

Tangerine Quartz

Carnelian

Crystals for Creativity

I have always considered myself to be a very creative person, but there have been periods in my life where I have felt disconnected from my creativity. These Crystals can help you connect or reconnect with your creative side.

Picture Jasper

Herkimer Diamond

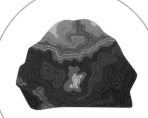

Bloodstone

Ulexite is an exciting Crystal for inner visions, imagination, and creativity. It brings about new ideas and keeps the inspiration flowing so that you can embark on new projects or complete one that you are having trouble with. Have a piece of Ulexite around to keep your imagination flowing, especially if you are trying to come up with new business ideas.

Tangerine Quartz balances the Sacral Chakra, which is the center for pleasure, passion, and creativity. It also brings about energy that stimulates inspiration and imagination. If you are having trouble jump-starting a project or getting through a creative block, Tangerine Quartz is the Crystal you need. When meditating, place a Tangerine Quartz near your Sacral Chakra, located about two inches below the navel, to activate and bring about creativity.

Carnelian is the ultimate Crystal for creativity. If you are looking to tap into fresh motivation and inspiration, then you ought to work with Carnelian. Not only does it balance your Sacral Chakra but it also brings new life to any creative project, and gives you the confidence to try new ideas and go in new directions. While working on a creative project, keep your Carnelian next to you to keep the creative juices flowing.

Bloodstone is a great Crystal for creativity because it helps to eliminate self-doubt. When you want to create something, but have come across some creative blocks or insecurities that make you want to give up, Bloodstone can help you keep going. It can also bring you new ideas and inspiration through dreams. If you want to spark your creativity, put a Bloodstone on your nightstand and ask it to bring you new creative ideas.

Herkimer Diamond is known for its ability to amplify positive energy, energize, and enliven. It brings you new ideas and inspiration, and gives you the motivation and energy to start a project and follow it through to completion. It encourages you to do more things that bring you happiness, even if they're out of character. Program your Herkimer Diamond with positive affirmations such as: "Creativity comes naturally and easily to me. I am full of great ideas."

Picture Jasper is a Crystal for grounding and organizing your thoughts. If you have been having creative blocks because you have a lot on your mind, Picture Jasper will bring mental clarity. It is also a great Crystal for tapping into deep thoughts for new ideas and creativity. Picture Jasper also has beautiful earthy patterns that you can look at to awaken creativity in your mind. Gaze at it gently by squinting your eyes a bit and see what the patterns reveal.

Honey Calcite

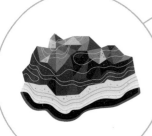

Amethyst

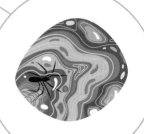

Amber

Crystals for Peace

Peace can mean different things to each person. There is internal peace, where everything in your life feels aligned; and there is external peace, such as peace on Earth. If you are looking to bring inner or outer peace, these Crystals can help.

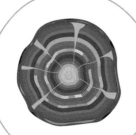

Iris Agate

Ajoite

Danburite

Amethyst is the ultimate Crystal for inner peace since it brings serenity and tranquility into any space. Simply staring at an Amethyst makes you feel more centered and at ease with any situation. Amethyst is also a Crystal for breaking negative patterns that are keeping you from your own inner peace. Place an Amethyst in your home where you can see it shine and it will illuminate any darkness that is getting in the way of your peace.

Honey Calcite transforms your mind by eliminating fear, self-doubt, and any dark energy that you might have from past experiences. Once you have eliminated these dark energies from your mind you can begin to embrace the naturally peaceful and nurturing energy of Honey Calcite. Pair Honey Calcite with other transformational Crystals such as Sapphire, Moldavite, Fluorite, and Ametrine while meditating to get rid of those pesky negative thoughts and achieve the peace you are looking for.

Amber is not actually a Crystal, but a tree resin that has fossilized over millions of years. It absorbs negative energy, heals emotional pain, and helps to get rid of fears and phobias. It clears your mind of negative thoughts and feelings and brings in positive energy like rays of sunlight. Wear Amber on your chest to not only bring you peace and happiness, but to extend those feelings to everyone who sees it, like a bright golden light.

Danburite is like a guardian angel inside of a Crystal. It helps you to connect with your passed loved ones and spiritual guides since it serves as a bridge between you and the angelic realms. It also helps eliminate stress, anxiety, fear, and anger. The next time you are feeling like you need a bit of spiritual guidance, hold your Danburite, close your eyes, and say a little prayer. Feelings of peace will flood over your entire body and soul.

Ajoite is a vibrant blue-green color usually found in Quartz. It is a rare, must-have, and powerful Crystal. Known as an emotional rescue Crystal, it brings peace, comfort, and nurturing to anyone who is going through a time of transformation. Use Ajoite in meditation when you want to release deep emotional feelings.

Iris Agate looks like a magical cave of rainbows. It helps you eliminate self-doubt, insecurities about yourself, and uneasiness about situations that are currently causing you anxiety. Once all of those inner obstacles are eliminated, peace can set in and everything can fall into place. Meditate with Iris Agate by holding a piece up to the Sun. As the sunlight illuminates its rainbows, look at every color and visualize yourself being enveloped by the peace that each light brings to you.

Black Obsidian

Blue Apatite

Citrine

Crystals for Motivation

We all need motivation to complete tasks, projects, assignments, and work. Without motivation, even the smallest task can seem impossible to endure. If you'd like to feel motivated, these Crystals can help you feel energized and ready.

Golden Topaz

Bronzite

Red Tiger's Eye

Black Obsidian is made when lava spews out of a volcano and dries without mixing with other minerals. This purity makes it one of the most powerful Crystals to absorb negative energy, emotional pain, and any memories and experiences that might be holding you back and preventing you reaching your full potential. If you are dealing with pain and grief, wear Black Obsidian daily for support.

Blue Apatite is a Crystal that can help you bring excitement back into your life. We all go through times when our everyday life becomes routine and there is nothing to look forward to, but Blue Apatite can balance your Throat Chakra so that you can express to your loved ones what will motivate and get you excited again. Put Blue Apatite in your car to stay motivated and clear as to where you want to go next.

Citrine is a popular Crystal because it does so much for the collective. It is known as "The Lucky Merchant Stone" because it brings good luck and wealth. It balances your Solar Plexus Chakra, which helps you step into your power and take charge of what makes you happy and motivated. Simply hold Citrine for a few minutes and you will feel its power. You won't want to put it down!

Red Tiger's Eye connects the energies of the Earth and Sun to help you rekindle passion for your artistic projects and responsibilities. If you have hit a wall and are feeling unmotivated, Red Tiger's Eye will help you reconnect with your natural skills, talents, and abilities. Wear Red Tiger's Eye when you are trying to find new vision for a project you began but stopped working on for lack of motivation.

Bronzite is a powerful eliminator of self-doubt. It reminds you that you can trust yourself and your life's purpose. With this trust, you will feel motivated and excited to keep going in the direction you want. Bronzite grounds, centers, and motivates you, like the voice of a guide or a mentor. Meditate with Bronzite the next time you need clarity on a decision or when you need an extra boost of motivation.

Golden Topaz helps direct energies to where they are most needed. It soothes and nurtures, but also ignites and gives you the courage to express yourself. It motivates you to follow your path and purpose and reminds you that you are the captain of your own ship. Wear Golden Topaz to your next formal dinner or celebration. You will feel like your best self and also motivate those in awe of your Golden Topaz energy.

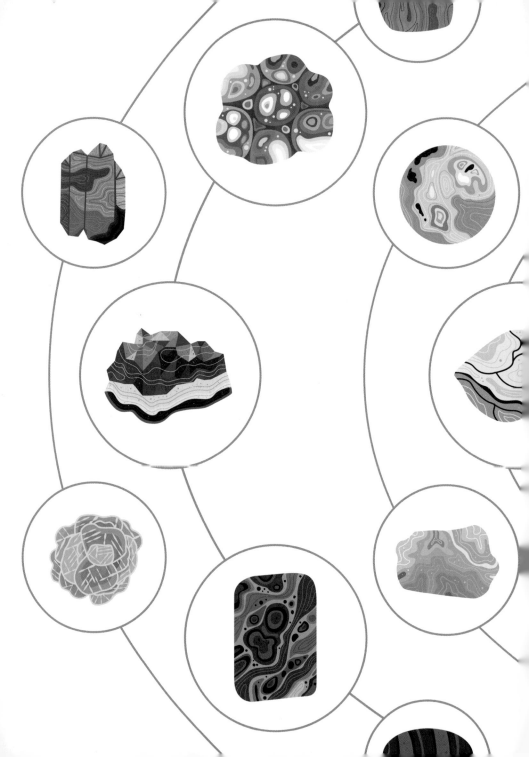

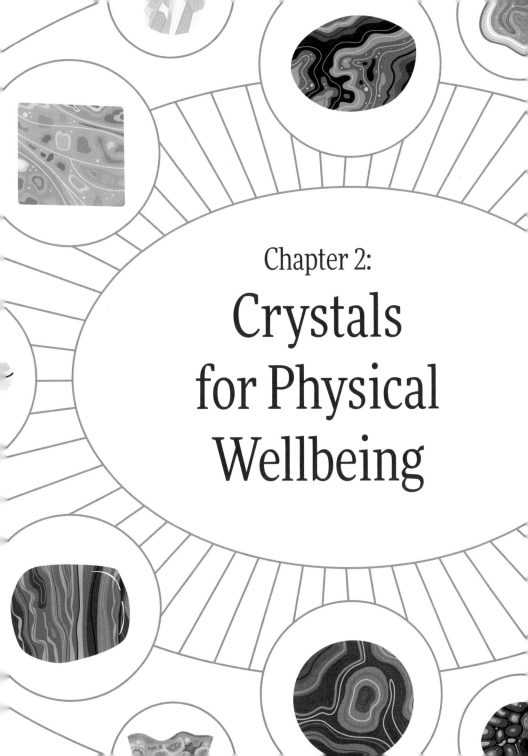

Chapter 2:
Crystals for Physical Wellbeing

Amethyst

Lepidolite

Angelite

Crystals for Better Sleep

The stresses of everyday life can keep you up at night, needing something to help calm your mind. If you are looking to work on this in your own life then these Crystals are for you.

Black Moonstone

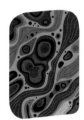

Leopard Skin Jasper

Selenite

Amethyst is one of the best Crystals to help you sleep better since it brings you tranquility, serenity, and can help quieten your mind. Amethyst will calm your stress levels with its soothing energy so that you are able to fall asleep quickly and wake up rested and refreshed. Simply put Amethyst on your nightstand or under your pillow to help with sleep, or place it in a bath before bed with a few drops of essential oils.

Lepidolite is known for its calming effects and is used for treating depression, anxiety, and other stress-related conditions. If you are having trouble turning off your brain at night Lepidolite can help you calm your thoughts and get to sleep quickly. Lay down with your Lepidolite and hold it in your receiving hand or up to your Third Eye Chakra. Close your eyes and take deep breaths. Slowly begin to visualize a purple light surrounding and calming you.

Angelite exudes a pillowy, warm, and loving energy. Named after angels, Angelite can help calm an overactive mind and help eliminate stressful thoughts that keep you awake. It can also help heal any emotional pain you might be feeling, which can prevent you from reaching the deep sleep you need for true rest and healing. Place Angelite anywhere in your room to receive its healing energy.

Selenite cleanses negative energy that has been trapped in a space and even absorbed by other Crystals. Placing Selenite in your bedroom will cleanse the space of any stagnant or negative energy left behind by inhabitants of the room, and even of negative emotions you might be having while you sleep. The energy in your bedroom will become purified, peaceful, and ready for healing. Place a Selenite in an elevated part of your bedroom where it can serve as an energy purifier for the entire space.

Leopard Skin Jasper is a very protective Crystal that brings positivity, stability, and strength in time of chaos. This is the perfect Crystal for people who deal with nightmares and have trouble getting restful sleep due to vivid dreams. Keep it close to your bed or sew it into a pillowcase to keep safe in your dreams. If you work with Leopard Skin Jasper more frequently it can help you remember your dreams and understand the messages they bring.

Black Moonstone is a rare Crystal because it is currently only found in Madagascar. Known for its protective qualities, it's great for balancing emotions and has the ability to radiate calming energy and clear the mind of stressful thoughts at night. This Crystal is especially useful for children and pregnant women. Create a restful sleep grid in your bedroom so that you may get right to sleep every night (see Chapter 7).

Desert Rose

Dream Quartz

Lodolite

Crystals for Good Dreams

Have you ever woken up tired because you dreamed all night and it felt as though you were awake? Or had vivid nightmares that woke you up? These Crystals can help ensure you have good dreams.

Hemimorphite

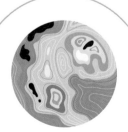

Rainbow Moonstone

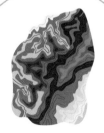

Moldavite

Desert Rose has a soft energy that helps you develop strength in who you are. It will enhance your dreams and bring clarity on their meaning, enabling you to recall them and closely reflect on their messages. Leave a Desert Rose and dream journal on your nightstand so that when you wake up, you can document your dreams with the energy of Desert Rose to help remember every detail.

Dream Quartz can stimulate lucid dreaming, where you can control what is happening in your dreams. It can also help you connect with spiritual guides to further your spiritual journey, and strengthen your psychic abilities. You may even begin to have prophetic dreams. To reap the full benefits of Dream Quartz, carry a piece with you while you are awake as well as asleep.

Lodolite is also known as Garden Quartz and Shamanic Dream Quartz because it can have the appearance of a city or even a garden inside. Used by shamans to help them journey to other worlds through sleep and dreams, Lodolite can be a great visualization and manifestation tool while you sleep. Before sleep, cleanse your Lodolite and ask it to record your night's dreams. When you wake up, sit and meditate with your Crystal. This should trigger enough memories for you to remember your dreams and receive their messages.

Moldavite is one of the most powerful Crystals. Created from the impact of a meteor hitting our planet, genuine Moldavite can only be found in the Czech Republic. Some believe that only a select few can handle Moldavite's high vibrational energy. Spend some time meditating with it and holding it before bringing it into your bedroom to help you with dream recall and to find the hidden messages in your dreams. You will soon feel that your energetic vibration has changed and that you feel stronger and more enlightened.

Rainbow Moonstone is known for its beautiful rainbow flashes of color. Holding a piece immediately makes you feel calm and serene, because it activates your Third Eye Chakra and Crown Chakra. Rainbow Moonstone helps you feel safe and secure by eliminating negative energy from your space so that you can fall into a deep sleep. Hold your Rainbow Moonstone before bed and allow it to activate your upper Chakras so that you can go into a relaxed and deep state of dreaming.

Hemimorphite is a Crystal of emotional healing and compassion. It allows you to express your truth and emotions. Once you have communicated your feelings you will be able to let go of any hurt or blockages those emotions might have been causing you. Wear your Hemimorphite and don't take it off until you feel you can easily remember and understand your dreams at night.

Smoky Quartz

Blue Calcite

Rose Quartz

Crystals for Relaxation

What comes to mind when you think of the word "relaxation?" For me, I instantly think about a spa day. But you can also experience relaxation from simply holding a Crystal. Here's some Crystals for bliss and relaxation.

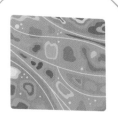

Grossularite

Kunzite

Magnesite

Blue Calcite is a wonderful Crystal for relaxation because it transmutes negative energy into positive energy, soothing nervousness and anxiety. Without frayed nerves and anxiety you can be a more grounded and happy you. Practice deep breathing while holding Blue Calcite and you will experience an instant calming and relaxing energy swoop all around your body.

Smoky Quartz is known for its protective qualities, and its ability to absorb negative energies by sending them down to be turned into positive energy by the Earth. Every time you begin to feel anxious, depressed, or lose focus, work with Smoky Quartz to help cleanse your aura and leave you feeling grounded, calm, and relaxed again. Smoky Quartz is also a great team player; mix it with Crystals that have different qualities you are looking for and wear them as a bracelet.

Rose Quartz is a Crystal for love, but it can also help you relax when you're feeling stressed. It is welcoming and nurturing, like that bestie who reminds you to put you first, neutralizing negative emotions so you can feel inner peace and have compassion for yourself. When you let go of stress, it's like you have taken a deep breath and exhaled into a state of relaxation. If you would like to feel relaxed, hold a Rose Quartz heart to your heart center and meditate with it, allowing its energy to relax every inch of your body.

Magnesite brings emotional calming and balance by supporting emotional healing. It helps you let go of fears that are blocking self-love, self-compassion, and even self-esteem, making you feel calm, creative, and in deep peace. This spiritual and emotional growth will allow you to relax again and live the life you deserve. Hold a piece of Magnesite while visualizing yourself at your best, to bring joy and relaxation back into your life.

Kunzite helps you to reconnect to and heal your inner child, allowing you to heal emotionally. One of the great qualities of being a child is the ability to relax instantly. When you let go like children do, you can feel joy, love, and relaxation. Wear Kunzite as jewelry to be reminded of how great it feels to let go, to not take things too seriously, and to make time for self-care and relaxation.

Grossularite is a well-rounded Crystal that helps you relax and live your best life. It promotes hope and empowerment by encouraging you to help others who are in need, teaching you that when you pay it forward, you will receive blessings tenfold. These actions can help your heart feel happy and fulfilled. Place a piece of Grossularite in your workspace to stimulate new ideas and bring peace and relaxation.

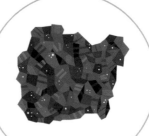

Vanadinite

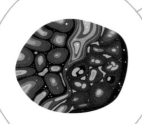

Fire Agate

Ruby Zoisite

Crystals for Energy

We all have days when it's hard to get out of bed, but Crystals can help reignite your physical, mental, and emotional energy. If you are looking to add pep to your step, these Crystals can help.

Tiger Iron

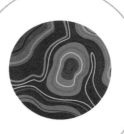

Carnelian

Brookite

Fire Agate is named after its hues of reds, browns, and golds. It has been mostly mined for jewelry but its energetic properties, which can help you feel level-headed, grounded, and fired up (hence its name) shouldn't be overlooked. Fire Agate also helps to revitalize, allowing you to tap into your stamina. The next time you're going to the gym, grab your Fire Agate and have a great workout!

Vanadinite has a beautiful and rare quality. Its fiery tones help you stay motivated to achieve your goals and make your dreams a reality. Use Vanadinite to keep your Root Chakra and Sacral Chakra—your centers for stability, abundance, and productivity—charged. Every morning, place a Vanadinite Crystal at these two Chakras and visualize it charging those centers for a more energized and productive day.

Ruby Zoisite is the perfect combination of Green Zoisite and Ruby. Together, they remind you that there is a whole world to explore; and to take the time to find the things that make you feel fulfilled. Ruby Zoisite gives you the energy to focus and make a relationship work. If you are currently working toward a romantic relationship or a business partnership, gift the other person a Ruby Zoisite so that you can both be in the same energetic playing field.

Brookite is a rare Crystal usually found in the matrix of other Crystals such as Albite, Rutile, and Quartz. Even though it is a small Crystal it packs a powerful punch, guiding you in your destined direction. Brookite has the ability to energize all of your Chakras and that extra boost can help you feel almost superhuman. If you are feeling fatigued or lethargic carry a piece of Brookite in your pocket to begin to feel its magic.

Carnelian has been used throughout history and in many cultures for its revitalizing properties. It has the ability to activate your three lower Chakras so that you will have the energy, courage, and motivation to follow your dreams and goals. Charge a jar of water with Carnelian by placing a Carnelian Crystal on top of a covered water jar with filtered water. Leave it for twenty-four hours and then drink it to recharge your body and give you energy.

Tiger Iron is a special Crystal containing the power of three dynamic Crystals: Tiger's Eye, Hematite, and Red Jasper. If you are feeling easily distracted or unmotivated, Tiger Iron can help you get back to feeling focused and creative. For best results say your daily affirmations while holding your Tiger Iron. This will energize your words so that they can become a reality. A great daily affirmation to use with Tiger Iron is: "I am energetic, healthy, creative, and determined. My greatness cannot be stopped!"

Yellow Jasper

Red Jasper

Shiva Lingam

Crystals for Sexual Energy

Sexual energy drives more than just sex since you can transmute this energy into passion and drive to succeed. These Crystals can help you have a healthy balance and connection with your sexual energy, for success in all areas of your life.

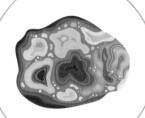

Fire Opal

Rubellite

Blue Tiger's Eye

Red Jasper can help revive sexual energy and bring back the desire to experience more passion and pleasure in a relationship. If you are in a long-term relationship, Red Jasper is the perfect Crystal to reignite that flame and bring newness back to a sexual relationship. Red Jasper is also great for finding a new passion that aligns with who you are. Wear Red Jasper daily to attract more people to you and have them see your authentic self.

Yellow Jasper boosts your self-confidence and self-esteem so that when you look in the mirror, you feel sexy and attractive. It can also increase your libido, sexual stamina, and overall physical performance. Yellow Jasper can also help you pick up new hobbies that require endurance and energy such as long-distance running. Place Yellow Jasper in your bedroom to help with stamina or carry with you when you engage in high-intensity activities.

Shiva Lingam is known for its elliptical shape. In Hindu culture, Shiva Lingam Crystals are the representation of the god Shiva's phallus and are known as a Crystal of sexuality, fertility, confidence, and balance. If you would like to connect to the power of Shiva Lingam, place one in your bedroom or carry a piece of it with you to help you feel more balanced, confident, and passion-driven.

Blue Tiger's Eye brings calming and grounding. If you have an overactive sex drive or sexual frustrations, Blue Tiger's Eye can help you find balance and release by reducing your anxiety and helping center your thoughts. It can also help you understand why you are wired the way you are. For protection, guidance, and better perspective, carry Blue Tiger's Eye with you until you feel you have reached a place of sexual energy stability.

Rubellite heals the Heart Chakra and activates the Root Chakra, bringing an increased flow of Prana (Life Force Energy), enthusiasm, and passion into your life. It can help revitalize passion and joy in sexuality, and can help bring the spark back into a sexual relationship. Put Rubellite under your bed to keep things fresh in the bedroom or place it at your workspace to be productive.

Fire Opal can help bring back joy into the hearts of those who are afraid to open up to loving and being loved. It can help you have a healthy relationship with your own sexuality so that you can have healthy sexual relationships with others. To get the most out of your Fire Opal, carry it with you in your pocket or wear it as jewelry. Remember to charge it under the Sun from time to time to keep it working at its fullest potential.

Green Calcite

Larimar

Clear Quartz

Crystals for Wellness

Wellness is the act of practicing healthy habits every day to achieve better physical and mental health outcomes. The Crystals on this page can help you achieve your wellness goals and help you reconnect with your own ability to heal.

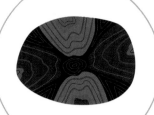

Chiastolite

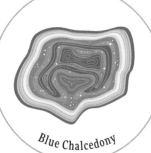

Blue Chalcedony

Rubellite

Green Calcite is the perfect all-around Crystal to help with physical and mental wellbeing. It brings healing and stability to your physical body (the lower three Chakras) and spiritual body (the higher three Chakras). It eases sadness, reduces stress, and promotes healthy and loving relationships by letting go and forgiving. Hold your Green Calcite to your heart center and visualize a beautiful green light illuminating your heart and cleansing it. This will clear anything in your Heart Chakra that is keeping you from achieving wellness

Larimar gets part of its name from *mar*, the Spanish word for the ocean. Its beautiful shades of blue are a reminder of the blue ocean and sky of the Caribbean where it is found. Holding Larimar, you surrender your stress, your worries, and any blockages in your Chakra system, especially the Throat Chakra. Place it under your pillow so that you can connect with its natural soothing and supportive wellness properties.

Clear Quartz is known as "The Master Healer" for its versatility and ability to act like any other Crystal. Once cleansed, you can program your Clear Quartz Crystal to do anything you'd like it to do. It can absorb negative energy and transmute it into positive energy, and also act as an amplifier when surrounded by positivity. When using it for wellness, cleanse it, and set your intentions and goals into it.

Rubellite is a Crystal of the heart and brings an increased flow of Prana (Life Force Energy). The ancient teachers believed that the flow of Prana through our bodies was directly connected to our overall health. Rubellite helps you directly work with this energy and the flow of it through your body. Hold your Rubellite through meditation or bring it with you during exercise classes to assist you with the flow of this energy.

Blue Chalcedony is one of the most nurturing and calming Crystals. It helps remove negative energy from your body, making it easier to connect with your own ability to heal and reach your wellness goals. It is also a great Crystal for mental wellness because it creates calm and peace and helps you balance your personal and professional life. To use it at its fullest potential, hold it when you are feeling anxious, sad, or just off.

Chiastolite is also known as "Fairy Crosses" because of the natural crystalline formations that create a cross-shaped marking on each Crystal. It can be used as an amulet of protection because it deflects negative energy, and is perfect for balance and self-improvement. It is believed that Fairy Folk have a link to Chiastolite and if you need their help and guidance, you can call on them by showing them the cross and they will come to your aid. To get the most out of Chiastolite, wear it, put it under your pillow, or decorate your fairy garden with a few small pieces.

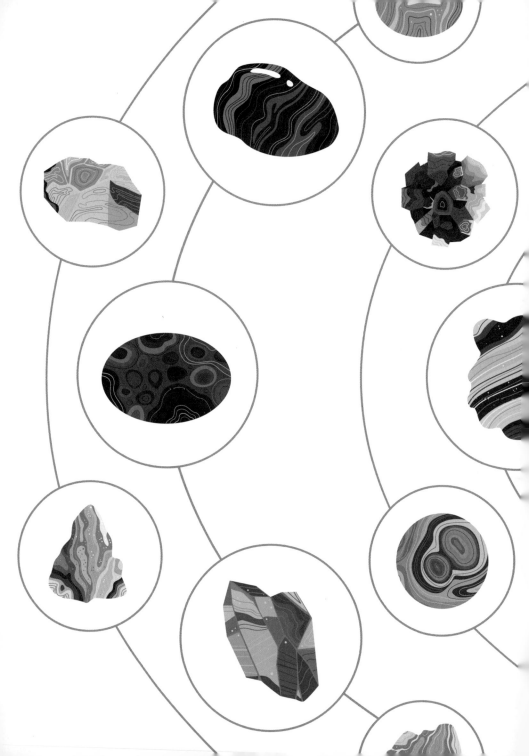

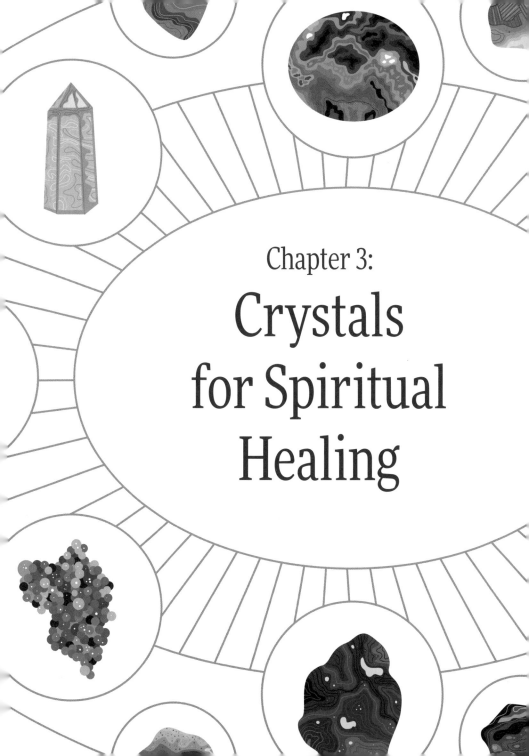

Chapter 3:
Crystals for Spiritual Healing

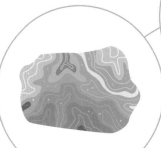

Rose Quartz

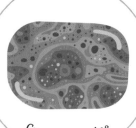

Green Aventurine

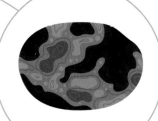

Rhodonite

Crystals for Self-Love

Make self-love a part of your daily life by taking care of your physical, mental, and emotional wellbeing. The Crystals on this page will help remind you to take a little time for you.

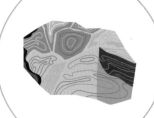

Morganite

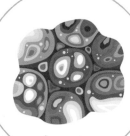

Lepidolite

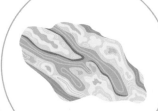

Pink Tourmaline

Rose Quartz is the Crystal for all kinds of love. When Rose Quartz starts to notice that you have depleted your inner love bank, it gently reminds you that it's time to slow down. It fills you up with warm and caring energy and gives your heart a little tug in the self-care direction. Rose Quartz's energy is so comforting yet so powerful that all you need to do is place it in the space you spend the most time in and let it do its work.

Green Aventurine helps you release and let go of old emotional traumas, opening your heart to receive new blessings and opportunities. Green is the color associated with the Heart Chakra, the center for emotional healing, and Green Aventurine wants you to experience any type of love that you need in your life, making it one of the best Crystals for putting you first! Place it anywhere near your heart center to feel its gentle and nurturing energy.

Rhodonite is one of the most powerful heart-healing Crystals. It can help you heal from emotional wounds and trauma, while also encouraging you to love yourself by seeking out what makes you feel good. Whether in big or small ways, Rhodonite will guide you to self-love. Like most self-love Crystals, wear Rhodonite near the heart center. You can also hold it during a facial appointment. In fact, Rhodonite is a great Crystal to hold during any self-care treatments because it exudes loving kindness, forgiveness, and promotes fresh starts, helping you feel good on the inside and outside.

Pink Tourmaline is a feminine energy Crystal. It is soothing, gentle, and comforting to the emotional body, and helps you release destructive feelings, guilt, worry, and negative thoughts. It brings compassion and uplifting energy, guiding you toward self-love so that you may do things that help you feel nurtured and cared for. Place a Pink Tourmaline near your heart but also at your front door so that only loving energy will enter your sacred space and home.

Lepidolite absorbs negative energy and replaces it with positive energy, compassion, and confidence. It reminds you that you are worth it, and gives you the mental and emotional tools to be positive and care for yourself. Hold your Lepidolite the next time you are feeling down. It will help absorb the low energy behind your thoughts and feelings so that you can see and feel clearly.

Morganite is a very rare Crystal that means business when it comes to heart healing in the gentlest of ways. It eliminates any blockages from your Heart Chakra so that energy can flow freely, pointing out the areas that might be causing you anger and resentment and stopping you from moving on. As you go through this healing process, Morganite holds your hand and is the friend who reminds you that everything you need is within you. Hold Morganite as you meditate to connect with divine love and guidance.

Citrine

Cinnabar

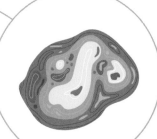

Gold

Crystals for Prosperity

Prosperity means something different to everyone. It can be about accumulating wealth and friends, or just having food and a safe place to live. Whatever prosperity means to you, the Crystals on this page can help you manifest and achieve that goal.

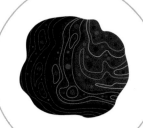

Tektite

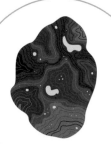

Blue Sapphire

Ruby

Citrine helps attract prosperity and abundance and is the perfect Crystal for prosperity because it transmutes negative energy into positive energy. It eliminates blockages, energizes, and helps you feel confident, meaning you are more likely to manifest your dreams. Put a piece of Citrine in your wallet with the purpose of attracting wealth.

Cinnabar is one of the most powerful prosperity Crystals. When people hear Cinnabar, they can sometimes be alarmed because it is known for being extremely toxic, since it contains Mercury Sulfide. However, unless ingested or inhaled it should be perfectly safe as long as you wash your hands after handling it. Cinnabar helps motivate you to follow your dreams and desires and also manifest any prosperity and abundance intentions. If you are a business owner, it is recommended that you add a small piece of Cinnabar in an airtight bag (to avoid skin contact) into your cash register to attract more sales for your business.

Gold may not be a Crystal, but it can truly bring prosperity into your life. It is believed in many countries and cultures that wearing Gold will attract more wealth and prosperity because it contains the Sun's energy. The Sun is the center of our solar system, and all the planets rotate around it, making it magnetic. In the same way, Gold is a magnet to attract only good things into your life. Carry a piece of Gold in your wallet, preferably a Gold coin, to attract wealth and prosperity.

Ruby gems have been known throughout history as the most valuable, even above Diamonds. Rubies can bring you vitality, power, and the energy to get things done. If you would like to invite more prosperity into your life by reaching the top of your career and work field, then try to carry a Ruby with you at all times.

Blue Sapphire is one of the best-kept secrets for manifesting wealth, luck, and prosperity. It helps protect you from negative energy that can prevent you from reaching your dreams, and also helps you accomplish life goals. Celebrities are known to use this Crystal for obtaining fame and fortune. Wear Blue Sapphire jewelry to attract prosperity into your life.

Tektite is the result of a meteor hitting the Earth. Tektite is very transformative because it strengthens your aura, raises your vibration, and removes any blockages from your lower three Chakras. When your lower Chakras are balanced and aligned, you can more easily find financial stability. Start by meditating for a few minutes while holding a piece of Tektite. If it helps you feel relaxed then you have the ability to connect with it but if it causes you to feel uncomfortable, you might not be ready to work with it.

Black Kyanite

Selenite

Spirit Quartz

Crystals for Aura Cleansing

Your aura is the electromagnetic field that surrounds your physical body like an energetic bubble. It is very important that you keep your aura protected and healthy. One of the ways to achieve this is by working with the following Crystals.

Herkimer Diamond

Larimar

Aqua Aura

Black Kyanite is shaped like a broom so is sure to sweep away any negative energy in your space. It creates an impenetrable bubble around your aura by eliminating negative energy and preventing negative thoughts. When you are feeling like you need an energetic cleanse, sweep your aura with a Black Kyanite. Envision the negative energy it's sweeping away going down into the earth and becoming renewed Earth energy.

Selenite is one of the most popular Crystals for cleansing. Ancient medicine systems believe that a person's aura is connected directly to their Chakras, and anything that will affect Chakras begins first in the aura layers. In the same way as you brush your hair, comb through your aura with a Selenite wand to cleanse it from any negativity and pollutants that might be hanging on to it.

Spirit Quartz carries a soft and calming energy, its tiny, cactus-like points bringing angelic and harmonious energy to any person or space. If you are feeling off or like you have absorbed other people's negative energy, sit in meditation for a few minutes as you hold a Spirit Quartz. Acknowledge any thoughts that come, and let them go. Then visualize the energy of the Spirit Quartz sweeping over your aura, and filling any cracks or holes in your aura. You've now shielded and repaired your aura!

Aqua Aura is a Quartz that has been paired with gold. This combination creates a high vibrational marriage, making it one of the best Crystals for aura cleansing. Aqua Aura not only connects you to your guides and other angelic dimensions, but it also has the ability to create a shield of light around your aura, protecting your aura so that nothing negative can get close to or past it. Wear it or keep it in the place where you spend the most time.

Larimar can help you release stress. When you are stressed, Chakras can become unbalanced, causing your aura to weaken. To cleanse your aura, wear Larimar and make sure it is touching your skin. Every time you wear your Larimar, envision beautiful blue water washing over your aura and cleansing away anything that no longer serves you. Visualize that anything the Larimar is washing away is going back into the ocean and being transmuted into renewed ocean energy.

Herkimer Diamond calls in powerful white light that cleanses and brings clarity. It is known for its high vibrational energy and its ability to help manifest anything you desire. It can help you develop your clairaudient, clairsentient, and clairvoyance gifts in order to perceive beyond what can typically be heard, felt, or seen. To create a shield of white light around your aura with a Herkimer Diamond, wear it as jewelry.

Sphalerite

Galena

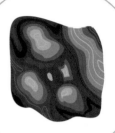

Mookaite

Crystals for Grounding

Do you ever feel that you are not connecting spiritually or like you cannot concentrate? Practicing grounding (connecting to Mother Earth) can help bring your thoughts back to this world and reduce stress. Here are some great grounding Crystals.

Polychrome Jasper

Hematite

Dumortierite

Galena brings your spiritual, etheric (aura), and physical body into balance, centering your energy and helping you feel grounded and alert. It gently anchors you to Mother Earth, facilitating your connection to her so that you can send the things in your life that are no longer serving you down to her to be transmuted into positive energy. Carry Galena with you so that you are always connected and feeling grounded.

Sphalerite is great for grounding when you have been working with high vibrational Crystals that have caused you to feel lightheaded or dizzy. It can help you feel like yourself again after meditation or deep healing work since it connects and balances your lower three Chakras, known as your physical Chakras. Keep Sphalerite around to hold and center yourself after meditation, yoga, Reiki sessions, or even a good workout at the gym.

Mookaite was named after the Indigenous Australian word *mooka*, meaning "running water," after the freshwater springs that feed the Australian region of Mooka Creek where it was first found. Mookaite is believed to be made up of microscopic remains of aquatic organisms (fossils), making it one of the best Crystals for grounding. Each piece is a part of Mother Earth's history and when you see it, touch it, and hold it, you are connecting with an intricate part of Earth's creation. Place Mookaite where you can admire it and be reminded of Mother Earth's beauty.

Dumortierite can help develop your psychic gifts and organize your thoughts and physical possessions. Make Dumortierite water by placing this Crystal on top of a purified water jar. Do not place it inside the water. Let it sit overnight and drink the water any time you want to feel balanced, grounded, and mentally strong.

Hematite acts like a magnet, pulling you into balance. It brings equilibrium and protects your physical, spiritual, and etheric body from negative energies. It also helps balance your feminine and masculine energies. Wear Hematite and make sure to let it touch your skin so that you may soak up all its grounding and protecting properties.

Polychrome Jasper was named because of its many colors. When you look at a Polychrome Jasper you are immediately reminded of Mother Earth's beauty, and can't help but feel connected to her. You can use this Crystal to revisit your earlier stages of life, healing any trauma or memories that are blocking your Root Chakra, the center for grounding. It takes longer to work than most Crystals, so leave it in a space where you won't have to move it and allow it time to slowly fill your space with earthy grounding energy.

Muscovite

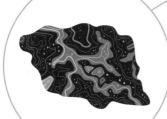

Chalcopyrite

Zebra Calcite

Crystals for Manifesting

Sometimes, it can be easier to believe that you can't have what you dream of, and that you should just be happy with what you have now. However, with intention and the help of the Crystals on this page, you can welcome anything into your life.

Tiger's Eye

Celestite

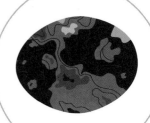

Healer's Gold

Chalcopyrite is an amazingly powerful Crystal for manifestation. Known as "The Mystic's Stone" it can bridge the gap between the spiritual and the physical worlds. Use it in your manifestation practice when you want to bring in new opportunities and wealth. Set your intentions very clearly into it and place it in any abundance Crystal grid (see Chapter 7) you might be setting.

Muscovite brings transparency into your life. It helps you see your toxic behaviors and relationships and the areas in which you need improvement. It clears your thoughts so that only positive thoughts can fill your mind and it gives you the confidence and trust in yourself to move forward. Muscovite creates the perfect emotional and mental balance to manifest successfully. Keep Muscovite nearby when writing your intentions so that you can be as clear and specific as possible.

Zebra Calcite is a Crystal that immediately begins to work with your emotional body. It balances your emotions and when you are having negative emotions and thoughts, it helps you sort through them in a gentle manner. When we don't believe good things will happen for us, they simply won't. Say daily positive affirmations such as: "I deserve every good thing to happen in my life" while holding your Zebra Calcite.

Healer's Gold is a rare Crystal that is highly coveted by light workers and healers, since it brings protection for those working closely with energy. Since Healer's Gold is made up of Pyrite and Magnetite, you get the powers of both. Pyrite can remind you of what you want in life, while Magnetite attracts it into your life like a magnet. Practice visualizing what you want to bring into your life daily while holding on to a piece of Healer's Gold.

Celestite encourages you to trust yourself and the universe. It is a Crystal for communication with the divine which makes it the perfect manifesting Crystal. It also gives you clarity of mind to speak your manifestations clearly into the universe. Celestite is a great addition to your bedroom because it brings relaxation and helps you remember dreams, which can be beneficial for processing messages from your higher self about your manifestations. Keep a dream journal next to your bed to jot down important messages in your dreams.

Tiger's Eye helps you feel grounded, motivated, courageous, and creative. Start a vision board to manifest what you want to attract to your life. Before getting started, spend a few minutes holding your Tiger's Eye since it will help you feel centered and allow you to come up with clear intentions. Then jot down your clear ideas and intentions for your vision board and get started!

Tanzanite

Grape Agate

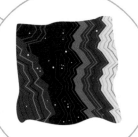

Lazulite

Crystals for Intuition

Have you ever been in a situation you instantly didn't feel good about it? Or felt something in your gut that told you to stay away? This is better known as your INTUITION and these Crystals will help you listen to it.

Merlinite

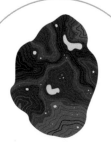

Blue Sapphire

Shattuckite

Tanzanite is 1,000 times rarer than diamonds, and the darker the color, the more valuable it is. All Tanzanites help you balance your Third Eye Chakra, but indigo Tanzanites especially helps you trust and strengthen your intuition. Wear Tanzanite jewelry so that you can tap into your psychic and intellectual abilities and learn to trust that little voice inside of you.

Grape Agate carries the energy of wisdom and growth, encouraging you to go within and find all the answers you seek. This makes it the perfect Crystal to tap into your intuition. When you have a question that needs answers, sit in meditation while holding your Grape Agate and see if you feel, hear, and see anything.

Lazulite helps you balance your Third Eye Chakra and attune to high vibrational energies. It helps strengthen your intuition by bringing insight into the answers you are looking for, and helps you see things more clearly by relieving you of the worries and fears you might have. Place your Lazulite at the center of your forehead before bedtime and ask it to help you receive the answers you are seeking while you sleep.

Shattuckite, known as "The Stone of Intuition and Psychic Abilities," helps you get in touch with your mind, body, and soul. It brings clarity when you feel confused or indecisive about something in your life, and will help you feel more at ease trusting your feelings. Use Shattuckite when you need to communicate something clearly to another person, such as when you are setting boundaries in a relationship.

Blue Sapphire is regarded as one of the most powerful Crystals of all time. One of the biggest benefits it possesses is that it brings peace and focus to the mind. Blue Sapphire helps you balance your Third Eye, which is your center for awareness, perception, and intuition. Look into your Blue Sapphire for answers. You will see that inside it is like deep waters and even if you don't see anything physically, it will help you go within to get in touch with your intuition.

Merlinite was named after the wizard, Merlin, and has the ability to attract magical experiences and good luck. It helps you connect with the light and dark within, helps you face your fears and worries, and gives a better understanding of who you really are. It encourages you to be more open to receive messages from spirit guides and the angelic realms. This is a rare Crystal to obtain and if you get your hands on a piece, simply carry it with you and watch it work its magic!

Aragonite

Ammonite

Red Jasper

Crystals for the Root Chakra

Chakras are centers of energy in our body containing our psychological, emotional, and spiritual states of being. First is your Root Chakra, one of three physical chakras, associated with the color red and located at the base of your spine. It is your center for basic needs and instincts. These Crystals can help you balance and heal this Chakra.

Unakite

Smoky Quartz

Jet

Aragonite, when held, can help you feel instantly grounded, making it one of the best Crystals for balancing the Root Chakra. When your Root Chakra is unbalanced, you can feel unsafe, unstable, and disconnected. Place an Aragonite at your Root Chakra for a few minutes while you relax and let it help you feel grounded and secure in yourself again. Aragonite will help you feel strong and resilient.

Ammonite is the fossil of extinct marine molluscs called ammonoids. Their spiral shells draw in negative energy and transmute it back out as positive and renewed Earth energy. Ammonites bring balance to the Root Chakra by stimulating your survival instincts and the will to persevere. They also encourage you to seek and achieve inner strength and personal power, both part of what a balanced Root Chakra will produce.

Red Jasper is a Crystal of personal strength, endurance, and stamina. It cleanses the Root Chakras of any blockages and activates it so that you feel grounded, energetic, and ready to conquer the world. Since the Root Chakra is correlated to sexuality in men, it can also help awaken, restore, and rejuvenate passion in men, physically or mentally. Wear Red Jasper jewelry to cleanse, balance, and activate your Root Chakra.

Jet is a potent cleanser and protector against negative energy. It helps you balance your Root Chakra by removing any blockages you might have there, leaving you feeling lighter and happier. When blockages are removed from your Root Chakra you will start to feel motivated and ready to accomplish anything you set out to do. To receive the energetic power from Jet, wear it as a necklace or carry it in your pocket.

Smoky Quartz is known for being very grounding and protective, yet gentle. It absorbs negative energy, protecting your auric field. It can also help relieve stress and anxiety, which can be an indication of an imbalance in this Chakra. Place a Smoky Quartz on your Root Chakra and visualize it cleansing and absorbing any blockages.

Unakite helps you to process the past and let go of negative habitual thoughts and inner dialogues. It reminds you that you deserve to feel happy, secure, and safe. Meditate with Unakite and visualize roots growing from your spine and into the ground. Once you have made this connection, send your negative thoughts and anything that no longer serves you down into the earth through the Root Chakra, to be transmuted into positive energy.

Tangerine Quartz

Peach Moonstone

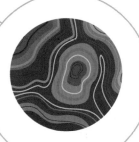

Carnelian

Crystals for the Sacral Chakra

The Sacral Chakra is your second Chakra, and the second of your physical Chakras. Associated with the color orange and located two inches below the navel, it is your center for emotions, relationships, and creativity. These Crystals can help you balance your Sacral Chakra.

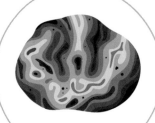

Copper

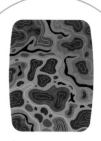

Brecciated Jasper

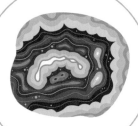

Agatized Coral

Tangerine Quartz is one of the best Crystals for balancing the Sacral Chakra because it increases joy and happiness by carrying you out of low moods. It is revitalizing, helps to make you feel rejuvenated and energetic, and sparks creativity so that you can get past creative blocks. Place Tangerine Quartz at your Sacral Chakra during meditation to receive its full benefits!

Peach Moonstone exudes gentle, feminine, and soft energy. It is great for balancing the Sacral Chakra because it helps you get back in tune with the rhythms of your body. One of the indications of a blocked Sacral Chakra is exhaustion. Peach Moonstone can bring you back to feeling refreshed and energetic by eliminating energy that is stuck in your body, allowing it to flow freely. Pair your Peach Moonstone with a Rainbow Moonstone to bring extra feminine healing to your body.

Carnelian is my favorite Crystal to use when I'm needing a boost of creativity. Egyptian warriors wore Carnelian to be victorious and get a boost of courage and confidence. You can use Carnelian to balance your Sacral Chakra by using it to help you feel confident, creative, energetic, sensual, and courageous. If you are looking to balance the Sacral Chakra with Carnelian, wear it in any form of jewelry.

Agatized Coral is a fossil with amazing properties. When you have a blocked Sacral Chakra, you can feel emotionally and physically weak. Due to the slow and enduring process Agatized Coral goes through to become fossilized, it is a powerful, stabilizing healer. It also helps you embrace positive changes in your personal life. Schedule self-care time and bring Agatized Coral with you to help you feel like yourself again.

Brecciated Jasper is a rare find—however, if you can find a piece you will not regret it! Brecciated Jasper is known as a Crystal of strength and vitality, which is why it's perfect for balancing the Sacral Chakra. It is also great for feeling grounded, emotionally stable, and clear-headed. Meditate with Brecciated Jasper when you are feeling emotional, for clarity and peace of mind.

Copper is used for balance and for facilitating an even flow of energy. An overactive Sacral Chakra can cause you to feel emotions more deeply, experience mood swings, be sexually aggressive, and be dissatisfied with life. Copper can help you ground these energies so that you no longer experience too much or too little. Wear Copper jewelry to maintain and balance your Sacral Chakra.

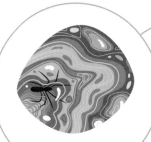

Amber

Bumblebee Jasper

Golden Topaz

Crystals for the Solar Plexus Chakra

The Solar Plexus is your third Chakra and the last of the three physical Chakras. Located from the navel to the diaphragm and associated with the color yellow, it is your source of personal power and personality. Use the following Crystals to balance your Solar Plexus.

Lemon Quartz

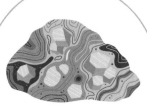

Pyrite

Honey Calcite

Amber is a fossilized tree sap used for its amazing warming properties. When you have a blocked Solar Plexus Chakra you don't feel confident, and Amber helps you to reconnect with your confidence and remember your worth. Get an amber pendant and visualize yourself at your best, shining in front of others. Set those intentions into the pendant and every time you wear it you will feel confident and charismatic.

Bumblebee Jasper raises your self-esteem and eases the stress that comes with worrying over others' opinions. When your Solar Plexus Chakra is blocked, you can lose your ability to feel confident and comfortable in front of others. This is no way to live! Place a Bumblebee Jasper at your Solar Plexus while laying down for at least five minutes and let it rebalance this center.

Golden Topaz brings a warm and nurturing energy just like the Sun, and has the ability to clear and protect you from negative energy. It brings its owner self-confidence, creativity, and inspiration without caring too much about others' opinions. Wear Golden Topaz jewelry in your receiving hand. This will ensure that you soak up all of Golden Topaz's energy.

Honey Calcite might look soft and sweet, but it is so powerful it can balance the Solar Plexus Chakra. It also brings you clarity and focus, allowing your mind to make better decisions and see that you are needed and important. Place Honey Calcite in the bathroom so that when you get ready you can see your true power and beauty right there in the mirror.

Pyrite got its name from the Greek word for fire, *pyr*, because it emits a spark when struck with Iron. Pyrite also lights a fire within you when you work with it energetically. When the Solar Plexus Chakra is blocked you may feel unsure of yourself and let others direct your life. Pyrite is here to spark joy again and to give you the strength to stand up for yourself. Consider placing Pyrite where you want to be reminded of your inner strength, perhaps where you start each day, such as in your car or next to your office computer.

Lemon Quartz can help balance the Solar Plexus Chakra because it is a Crystal of empowerment and optimism. It empowers you toward self-love and self-worth and it removes self-doubt. When you have a Lemon Quartz near you it can also naturally help to eliminate negative energy from your Solar Plexus Chakra so that it stays balanced. If you feel this Chakra is blocked, take a few minutes to lie down. Place a Lemon Quartz at your Solar Plexus Chakra, close your eyes, and visualize its bright yellow light entering this center. Imagine it cleansing this Chakra and allowing the energy to flow easily again.

Vivianite

Green Opal

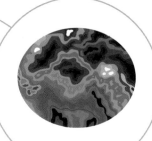

Moss Agate

Crystals for the Heart Chakra

The Heart Chakra is your fourth Chakra. Located at the center of the chest, it is associated with the colors green and pink and is a source of love for yourself and others. These Crystals can help keep this Chakra balanced and activated.

Fuchsite

Watermelon Tourmaline

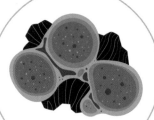

Prehnite and Epidote

Vivianite is a Crystal of love, compassion, and peace that can connect to the goodness in your heart. It can help remove negativity from your mind, body, and aura so that you can begin to feel the love for people and things that you may have lost over time, as well as find joy in the simple things again. This powerful Crystal should not be exposed to light for too long, but worked with in meditation and then wrapped in silk and put away.

Green Opal is the perfect Heart Chakra Crystal because it helps cleanse and rejuvenate the emotions of anyone who is suffering from sadness and heartbreak. Green Opal helps you open up, feel optimistic, and start rebuilding. Pair Green Opal with other Heart Chakra Crystals such as Rhodonite or Rose Quartz (see page 58-9, Crystals for Self-Love) to help cleanse and open up the Heart Chakra.

Moss Agate eliminates any negative energy from your heart center so that positive energy can flow freely and easily. It also helps you nurture all of your friendships and love relationships so they are strengthened and cultivated. Allow Moss Agate to bring you peace and harmony by setting it on your nightstand.

Prehnite and Epidote are a heart-healing super team. Prehnite alone has the ability to connect your Heart Chakra to your Solar Plexus Chakra, which is important for those trying to increase their self-esteem and self-love. Epidote, on the other hand, is an amplifier of positive energy, increasing the energy of unconditional love, compassion, and self-forgiveness. Together they make great companions to bring when you go to any healing session that requires you to express yourself from the heart.

Watermelon Tourmaline is known for its ability to unlock, cleanse, and eliminate energy blocks in your Heart Chakra. It encourages you to nurture yourself through acts of self-love and increases self-confidence, sympathy, and empathy. Wear Watermelon Tourmaline jewelry the next time you want to work on balancing your Heart Chakra.

Fuchsite cleanses the heart and soul through its hopeful, serene, and nurturing energies. Most importantly, Fuchsite can help you heal from trauma and pain caused by past relationship so that you can move on and be able to love wholeheartedly in new relationships. Place Fuchsite on any windowsill of your home so that its energy fills your home and you are able to maintain an open Heart Chakra.

Aquamarine

Arfvedsonite

Chrysocolla

Crystals for the Throat Chakra

The Throat Chakra is your fifth Chakra and the first of three spiritual Chakras. Associated with the color light blue and located at the center of the neck, its functions are expression, truth, and manifestation. The following Crystals can activate this center for communication.

Amazonite

Blue Lace Agate

Caribbean Calcite

Arfvedsonite brings mental clarity so that you are able to understand what you want and express it clearly. It helps remove any blockages in your Throat Chakra by removing self-doubt and negative thoughts. As Arfvedsonite helps you communicate, you are able to manifest more powerfully. When manifesting, hold an Arfvedsonite Crystal and speak out your intentions with confidence.

Aquamarine encourages clarity of mind and purity of heart so that you can speak from a place of love, while being mindful of the power your words carry. Aquamarine has long been regarded throughout history as a Crystal of peace, tranquility, and communication. Wear Aquamarine as close as possible to your Throat Chakra so that you can always find the correct words to say and to prevent arguments or misunderstandings.

Chrysocolla is perfect for people who have a hard time communicating their feelings. It connects your Throat Chakra and your Heart Chakra so that you can speak from a place of love. When working with Chrysocolla, you will feel more confident in the messages you are trying to convey. Chrysocolla also helps you communicate in a positive manner with people who can come off as aggressive or intimidating. Place Chrysocolla in rooms where you do a lot of communicating.

Caribbean Calcite catches your eye because it looks like Mother Earth took a picture of the beach and printed it on a Crystal. Just like the beach, it brings peace and tranquility so that you can communicate with ease. Caribbean Calcite helps you express yourself openly and authentically. Place a small tumbled piece of Caribbean Calcite on your Throat Chakra to cleanse it and help get the energy flowing.

Blue Lace Agate has been used throughout history as an amulet of peace and protection. Today we know it for its ability to cleanse and activate our Throat Chakra, allowing us to express ourselves. It is a reminder that you deserve all of the things you desire. Blue Lace Agate will help you feel like what you have to say does matter and that you should be heard. Pair Blue Lace Agate with self-love Crystals, such as Rose Quartz or Rhodonite, for an extra boost of confidence.

Amazonite has a deep connection to the water element and inspires the flow of energy and inspiration. It will help you communicate creatively, so it's perfect for people who speak for a living, such as singers, comedians, actors, motivational speakers, and teachers. Wear it as jewelry when you need your communication to flow freely, harmoniously, and creatively.

Euclase

Cavansite

Kyanite

Crystals for the Brow Chakra

The Brow Chakra, or the Third Eye, is your sixth Chakra and the second of the spiritual Chakras. Associated with dark blue and located at the center of the forehead, it reveals insights about the future by developing your intuition. The following Crystals will balance this Chakra.

Dumortierite

Lapis Lazuli

Barite

Euclase helps amplify your psychic abilities so that you are more in tune with your intuition and are able to follow your gut. One very special quality about Euclase is that it will connect your heart to your intuition so you can listen to your heart without ignoring red flags. Allow Euclase to balance your Brow Chakra by placing it directly at the center of your forehead. Visualize its blue color cleansing and reenergizing your Third Eye.

Cavansite is an extremely rare Crystal that stands out because of its electric blue rosettes. One of its most important properties is that it helps you decipher what your dreams mean. Leave a piece of Cavansite on your nightstand as you sleep to get better at seeing the meaning and messages behind your dreams.

Kyanite is one of the very few Crystals that does not absorb negative energy and therefore does not need to be cleansed. It protects you from negative energy by entering your auric field and shielding your Chakras. Work with Kyanite when you want to balance your Third Eye. Before bedtime, speak your intention into your Kyanite about the messages you'd like to receive while you sleep.

Barite has amazing Third Eye properties. Part of balancing your Third Eye is being able to connect with the spirit world. Barite helps you reconnect with your ancestors, guides, and higher self. You can sometimes carry your ancestors' pain and Barite teaches you that it's ok to let go and release love so you can go on feeling happy and fulfilling your life's purpose. Place a piece of Barite in any room you spend a lot of time in to receive its gentle yet transformational energy.

Lapis Lazuli has been used throughout history by royalty because of its immense power. It opens and activates your Third Eye Chakra to receive wisdom and see beyond what the naked eye can see. When you are ready to receive the wisdom of your Third Eye, create a Lapis Lazuli grid and set your intentions. Read more about Crystal gridding in Chapter 7.

Dumortierite helps you feel connected and grounded to Mother Earth. Although many are curious to open their Third Eye, it is recommended that you work on your three physical Chakras first so that you have a strong foundation and aren't inviting any ill-meaning energies into your space. Dumortierite keeps you focused and helps you expand your mind so that when you begin to receive visions and messages you will know what to do with them. This is the perfect Crystal for people with psychic abilities because it expands your mind yet keeps you centered. Pair Dumortierite with Clear Quartz to amplify its energy, enabling it to bring clarity and balance to your Brow Chakra.

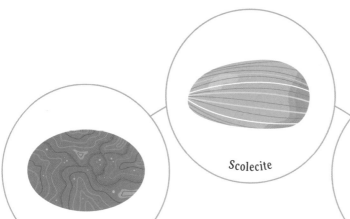

Scolecite

Ametrine

Angelite

Crystals for the Crown Chakra

The Crown Chakra is your seventh Chakra and the third spiritual Chakra. Associated with purple and located at the top of your head, it helps connect you to the spiritual world, increase motivation, and develop self-worth. Use these Crystals to balance and heal your Crown Chakra.

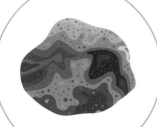

Peacock Ore

Auralite 23

Labradorite

Angelite helps balance your center for spirituality—your Crown Chakra—by improving your spiritual awareness and dispelling fear. Angelite is the best Crystal for angelic connection. It removes everything from your life that works to separate you from the spiritual world—anxiety, fears, and resentment—allowing you to balance your Crown Chakra. Simply hold your Angelite, take a few deep breaths, and sit in a few minutes of silence to activate your Crown Chakra.

Scolecite is a wonderfully soothing and gentle Crystal that helps calm the mind and remove blockages caused by worries. Once it has helped you reach clarity and peace of mind, you are able to rest, physically and emotionally. Place a Scolecite under your pillow to soothe your mind and receive messages from your guides and angels as you sleep.

Ametrine removes blockages at the Crown Chakra by bringing harmony, clarity, and releasing negative emotional programming and expectations. It brings joy and sunshine into your life, making it easier to see the beauty in everything, which is one of the Crown Chakra's basic functions. Wear Ametrine daily to keep your Crown Chakra balanced.

Labradorite is known as "The Stone of Transformation" because it brings out the best in you, empowering you and helping you feel self-confident. It helps calm an overactive mind by relieving stress and anxiety. Labradorite is the perfect Crystal to balance the Crown Chakra because it connects you both to the magic from other realms and to the magic within. Hold Labradorite in meditation and set your intention to connect to your higher self, which has all the answers you need to live your best life!

Auralite 23 is named after the twenty-three minerals it contains, which are what makes it so powerful and rare. Auralite 23 accelerates spiritual transformation, psychic abilities, lucid dreaming, and connection to the angelic realms. It can help balance your Crown Chakra so that you may manifest anything. Keep Auralite 23 at hand to give your manifestations a powerful boost.

Peacock Ore is a nickname given to the Crystal Bornite. Its colorful spectrum is a reminder that there is true beauty even in the smallest of things and that life is too short to dwell on the past. Peacock Ore helps you release regrets, traumas, grudges, and anything blocking you from reaching a higher dimension of spirituality and consciousness. Place Peacock Ore at the top of your head during meditation and visualize purple light emanating from the Crystal, creating a protective shield around your entire body.

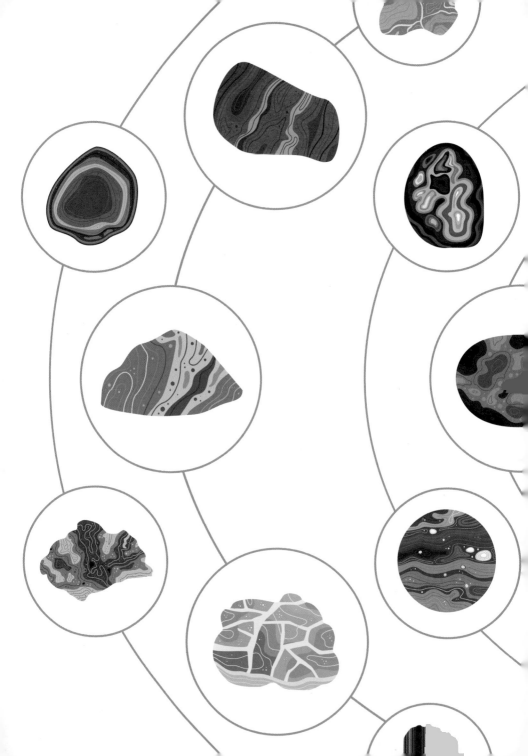

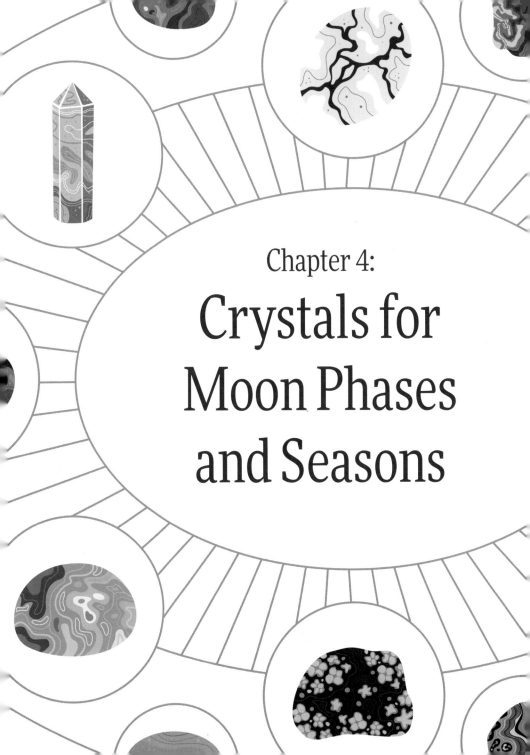

Chapter 4:

Crystals for Moon Phases and Seasons

Smoky Quartz

Rhodonite

Lapis Lazuli

Crystals for the New Moon

Crystals can help you harness the magical energy of the Moon. The New Moon is the first phase of the Moon cycle and a perfect time to start afresh and to set your intentions for new beginnings. These Crystals can help you plant the seeds of new ideas and projects.

Pink Opal

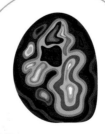
Labradorite

Black Obsidian

Smoky Quartz can pick up all the old energy you are carrying around and transform it into positive energy to manifest your heart's desires. The New Moon is the perfect time to start afresh and drop anything that no longer serves you. Run a Smoky Quartz around your aura to pick up and cleanse any energy you no longer need.

Rhodonite is a Crystal that helps you to gently reflect upon and evaluate where you stand in your life, what is working, and what no longer works, so you can decide what will stay and what will go in the next cycle. Keep Rhodonite near as you journal and write out your New Moon intentions.

Lapis Lazuli helps see clearly what you can let go of and what is missing in your life. Sometimes you may struggle with the idea of shedding parts of yourself that you no longer need, and if you feel resistant to working with Lapis Lazuli, you might be holding on to something that isn't good for you. Take a moment to meditate with Lapis Lazuli to give yourself an honest and truthful look at yourself. This will be so powerful starting anew for this cycle.

Black Obsidian is a Crystal of protection, and it serves as a mirror for you to do some self-reflection. Stare into Black Obsidian and what do you see? This Crystal will help clear any energies that may prevent you from being fruitful during the Moon's cycle. It will also help you to feel grounded and clear-headed.

Labradorite helps to illuminate your life so you can find your true meaning and gather up your thoughts. One origin story of this Crystal tells of an Inuit warrior who believed the Aurora Borealis lights were trapped inside Labradorite Crystals. When he struck them with his spear the lights were released, but some remained in the Crystal. Wear Labradorite while doing your New Moon rituals so that you can manifest more powerfully.

Pink Opal is the perfect Crystal for releasing old traumas, negative emotions, and healing wounds. In order to harness New Moon energy at its fullest you first must leave behind old wounds, forgive yourself, and have a fresh start in mind. Pink Opal lovingly encourages you to move forward, releasing any guilt you might feel. It also helps you feel at peace with your decisions, making the perfect environment for manifesting all of your desires. Have a Pink Opal nearby when writing out your New Moon manifestations to help bring calmness and clarity.

Green Opal

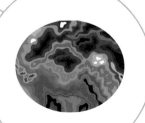

Moss Agate

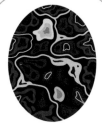

Green Aventurine

Crystals for the Waxing Moon

During the Waxing Moon phases (the Waxing Crescent and the Waxing Gibbous), the Moon is growing. During these phases you will feel in tune with your emotions, motivated, and hopeful. Take advantage of this illumination phase with the following Crystals.

Howlite

Sodalite

Fluorite

Green Aventurine is known as "The Gambler's Stone" because it brings you good luck and the motivation to take risks. Have you ever watched people playing craps in a casino? They roll the dice with enthusiasm and cheer and high five each other when they win. When they lose they still cheer each other on and move on quickly, not letting one loss stop them from having fun. In the same way, use Green Aventurine energy during the Waxing Crescent phase to take chances and follow your dreams. Pick out a small Green Aventurine you can carry around as your lucky stone.

Green Opal is a Crystal of strength and perseverance. Use it during the Waxing Crescent phase to push forward and build your plans for success. It will help you get rid of any fears you might have around your dreams so you're not in the way of your own success. Leave a Green Opal out overnight to be charged with the energy of motivation and perseverance.

Moss Agate will help stabilize your emotions so they don't cloud your judgment. During the Waxing Crescent phase you will feel extremely in tune with your emotions, so it is important that you work with this stone. Don't let the past stop you! Put the feelings of fear aside and tell yourself your dreams and goals have already happened. Wear Moss Agate as a reminder that you will achieve them.

Howlite is a Crystal of gentle motivation that will be your loving cheerleader! During the Waxing Gibbous phase you may start to get sidetracked, or feel discouraged that you aren't as far along in achieving your New Moon goals as you had hoped. Instead of giving up, get ahold of your Howlite Crystal. Go back to the drawing board to tweak your original plan to fit it into your current situation.

Fluorite is a great Crystal for the Waxing Gibbous phase. Fluorite helps you learn, focus, and concentrate, and also alleviates the stress around these activities. When you are trying to accomplish your goals, sometimes you can get distracted and lose focus, drive, and motivation. Adding Fluorite to your space will keep you centered and focused on your intentions.

Sodalite encourages rational thinking. If you're feeling helpless or like you haven't accomplished what you set out to, remember all it takes is a little editing of your plans and intentions and you can still be on the way to manifesting what you wanted at the beginning of this lunar cycle. Sodalite will help you find the motivation to keep going. Don't be afraid to ask for help and express your emotions and feelings, whether it's on paper, or with a friend or even a spiritual guide.

Clear Quartz

Rainbow Moonstone

Snowflake Obsidian

Crystals for the Full Moon

The Full Moon phase is the best time for getting clarity on what is and is not serving you, and the most powerful time to manifest with and charge your Crystals. The following Crystals can help you through a power-packed Full Moon.

Rose Quartz

Chrysocolla

Shungite

Rainbow Moonstone aligns you with the power of the Moon and can make sure you are balanced and plugged in to the Moon's intense energy so that you are not feeling out of sorts. It can also help eliminate any toxins and negative energy trapped in your auric field and physical body. Wear Rainbow Moonstone during the Full Moon phase to avoid the negative effects of such powerful energy around you.

Clear Quartz can take negative energy in your space and transmute it into positive energy. It can also amplify any positive energy, making it a great Crystal to use for manifesting during the Full Moon. For example, you can write down your intentions on a piece of paper, fold it, put a piece of Clear Quartz on top, and leave it out overnight during the Full Moon to supercharge both. You can also create a Clear Quartz grid for manifesting (see Chapter 7).

Snowflake Obsidian helps you learn from your mistakes while ensuring you don't berate yourself for them. This is the perfect Full Moon Crystal because it helps you evaluate your current life with clarity of mind, and let go of the destructive patterns and bad habits that have been holding you back. Place Snowflake Obsidian at your door so that you can leave all of the negative patterns there.

Shungite has cleansing and purification abilities for your energy flow. The Full Moon phase is an important time for transformation and renewal. With the power of the Full Moon and Shungite you can ground and balance your energy and start anew with a simple bath ritual. Place Shungite Crystals in your bath and leave them for fifteen to twenty minutes, then remove the Crystals and get into your freshly purified bath. Don't forget to set your intentions for the Full Moon while in the bath!

Chrysocolla can support you when releasing old patterns and behaviors because it is soothing and comforting. It empowers you to accept the truth and it helps calm and balance your emotions for a smooth transition. Meditate with Chrysocolla by holding it up to your heart center. Close your eyes and allow its energy to fill your Heart and Throat Chakras, the centers for self-acceptance and self-expression.

Rose Quartz encourages you to care of yourself. Take a nice warm bath and place a Rose Quartz next to the bath to receive its nurturing and caring energy. You can also place a Rose Quartz on top of or beside a jar of water to charge the water and Crystal overnight and make Full Moon water. Drink the water the next day to receive self-loving energy, or make a spray. Please note that making Moon water is not recommended during Lunar or Solar Eclipses because of the extra added intensity in the energy.

Polychrome Jasper

Amazonite

Lepidolite

Crystals for the Waning Moon

The Waning Gibbous and Crescent phase is a good time to get rid of excessive things in your life and to reflect on what you are grateful for, ready to start afresh. The following Crystals can support you through this phase.

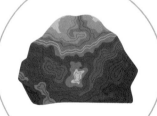

Bloodstone

Blue Calcite

Unakite

Amazonite helps you to naturally release blockages and negative energy, offering a reminder to make yourself a priority. Hold an Amazonite palm stone and ask it to easily and freely allow your body, mind, and spirit to release, then watch the negativity float away.

Polychrome Jasper helps you celebrate life and all its beauty, and calls you to embrace change. It brings excitement for what's to come and gets you thinking about what you will accomplish next. Pair it with other high-energy Crystals such as Citrine or Ruby so that you can begin thinking about your goals and manifestations for the New Moon cycle.

Lepidolite has the perfect energy for the Waning Gibbous phase, where you are called to reflect on the end of this Moon cycle. It helps you connect to your higher self, where you possess all of the answers to the difficult questions you have about yourself. It holds your hand while you deal with change and reorganize parts of your life that need tidying up. Wear, hold, or place Lepidolite near as you reflect on what you need to let go of now to make space for new blessings.

Unakite helps you stay strong emotionally and fills you with empathy, compassion, and forgiveness. The Waning Crescent Moon immediately precedes the beginning of a new cycle, like death and rebirth. It is time to evaluate and heal what's left of this old cycle so you can start afresh and be stronger than ever. Reflect while holding Unakite so that you know what parts of your emotional body need strengthening.

Blue Calcite transmutes negative energy into positive energy. It helps to cleanse your energy field of any unwanted energies, helping you to enter the New Moon cycle feeling ready to manifest all of your heart's desires. Blue Calcite also brings you clarity of mind and helps you express yourself clearly. Wear Blue Calcite into the New Moon cycle so that you can manifest and set your new intentions clearly and specifically.

Bloodstone is cherished for its physical and spiritual purification properties. A Crystal for overall wellness, it will help you clear away any negativity before you enter the New Moon cycle. It is also a stone of mental determination, and will help you come up with what you want to manifest next. Put Bloodstone under your pillow so that it can bring you healing as you sleep, and provide mental purification ready for your new endeavors.

Peridot

Emerald

Celestite

Crystals for Spring

As the darkness of winter diminishes and the day becomes longer than the night, you might begin to feel imaginative and creative. Plant your seeds in spring, celebrate new beginnings, and use the following Crystals to reset and restart *

Citrine

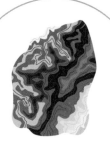

Moldavite

Smithsonite

Emerald holds the same energy as the process of spring. In spring we see life come back to Earth. There are new births, flowers bloom, birds chirp, and what was covered white in snow is now vibrant green. Emerald connects to your heart to bring you healing, renewal, vitality, and new life, just like spring does to Earth. If you are looking to start a new project, take up a new hobby, or learn a new trade during spring, wear Emerald jewelry, preferably close to your heart center.

Peridot is a reminder of the blooming flowers and plants that bring renewal and positivity to everyday life. It helps rescue relationships affected by grudges, misunderstandings, and negative thoughts by helping you release anything that is straining your relationships. Some relationships are better to let go of but some are worth fighting for. Gift Peridot to the person you are trying to make amends with as a token of your true friendship and a fresh new start.

Celestite can assist you through spring growth and development with ease and serenity. It is important to take some time during spring to go within and figure out how you want to grow and continue evolving during this important season. It also facilitates your connection to your guides and angels so you can call on them for guidance. Take some time to cleanse your Celestite and add a new intention for spring, such as: "This spring I intend to grow emotionally and spiritually by working hard at expressing my feelings and asking for help."

Smithsonite helps alleviate any depression, low energy, and anxiety you may have be struggling with during winter. In spring you may want to break out of your shell and step into happiness and light. Smithsonite can help you start afresh and find peace again. Place a piece of Smithsonite on your Third Eye Chakra, close your eyes, and sit in meditation for a few minutes. This will bring you clarity, heightened intuition, peacefulness, and awareness.

Moldavite can help you transform and evolve your heart center. Spring is the perfect time to grow and Moldavite can help you grow emotionally. Once you have acclimated yourself to its high vibration by spending time around it, you will find it is actually quite gentle. It helps you let go of fears and self-limiting beliefs. Place this Crystal at your heart center daily and watch yourself transform.

Citrine can hold the intention of anything you want to manifest this spring. Ask yourself: "What do I really want?" Once you have decided what you want to manifest, state it with complete confidence and belief that it will happen. Remember be clear and specific so you get exactly what you want.

* The advice on pages 94–101 is based on the Northern Hemisphere seasons, if you are in the Southern Hemisphere, just reverse it!.

Aquamarine

Ruby

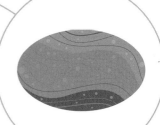

Orange Calcite

Crystals for Summer

Summer is about fun in the Sun. Waking up to a sunny morning can brighten anyone's mood. However, rising temperatures can sometimes bring out moodiness. The following Crystals will help you stay positive and balanced during such a supercharged time.

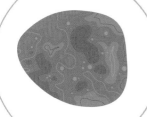

Sunstone

Larimar

Ocean Jasper

Aquamarine is the perfect Crystal for summer because it embodies the energy of a serene light-blue ocean. The name Aquamarine is derived from the Latin words *aqua*, for "water," and *marina*, meaning "of the sea." Just looking at this Crystal helps you feel instantly relaxed. Hold it to feel as though you are being carried away by the smooth waves, into a tranquil state of mind.

Ruby inspires adventures with friends and family. Whether it is to ride rollercoasters, go snorkeling, or have a salsa dancing date, Rubies support your every summer idea. This Crystal promotes passion, love, excitement, and makes you feel young. Go grab your rough- or gem-cut Ruby and make summer memories!

Orange Calcite and its bright color lights up any room just like the summer Sun. It brings instant joy and inspires creativity, sensuality, and willpower. It can also help you out of feelings of depression and sadness so that you can get out and live your best life. If you are looking to have fun this summer and feel energetic, place a piece of Orange Calcite on your Solar Plexus Chakra and allow it to cleanse and balance this energetic center.

Ocean Jasper is a Crystal of happiness, joy, and emotional stability. It comes in many shades including green, yellow, blue, gray, white, and pink. It can help to heal from traumas you may be carrying around, allowing you to feel whole again. This joyful energy is perfect for summer.

Larimar can help transport you to a beautiful island in your mind because it brings you mental agility, imaginative visions, and strength. It can also help dissipate feelings of stress and anxiety. Only found in the Dominican Republic, holding Larimar is like holding a piece of island paradise. Meditate while holding Larimar and picture yourself on white sands, even if just for a quick escape!

Sunstone brings new life into your emotional and physical body, giving you a battery-like recharge. What better Crystal than Sunstone for summer? Native American tribes in Oregon believed that Sunstone was created by the blood of an injured warrior falling on some stones, infusing them with courage and power. Carry your Sunstone with you and be filled with joy, freedom, and personal power.

Carnelian

Blue Apatite

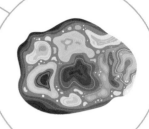

Fire Opal

Crystals for Fall

Fall is a wonderful time of abundance
and harvest. It's a time to enjoy holidays
and festivities that honor your ancestors
and remind you of all you have to be
grateful for. Use the following Crystals
to thrive and enjoy this season.

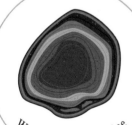

Watermelon Tourmaline

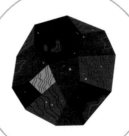

Garnet

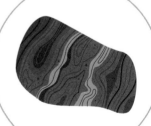

Red Jasper

Blue Apatite is a Crystal of motivation, mental strength, self-acceptance, and focus. Blue Apatite helps balance all of your Chakras, but especially your Brow Chakra (Third Eye). Blue Apatite opens up your creativity and ability to think outside the box. Place a Blue Apatite in a location where you are planning or creating for the fall celebrations ahead.

Carnelian contains shades of light to dark orange that are reminiscent of fall leaves. This vibrant Crystal will keep you energized, revitalized, and creative. It will bring you the courage to become the head of the planning committee or lead volunteer of the canned goods drive, and ensure that you are living your life to the fullest. Put a Carnelian in your pocket and tackle any project, big or small.

Fire Opal helps attract abundance, wealth, and prosperity. It is a Crystal of determination and passion and with its energy, you can succeed in anything you set your mind to. Place a Fire Opal in any space where the energy feels dull and give it a boost of fire energy to keep passion and creativity flowing.

Red Jasper helps you balance your emotional and physical energy. It is a great Crystal for grounding and clarity of mind. During this time of transition Red Jasper helps you feel comforted, centered, and grounded. It helps evaluate your personal happiness so that you can improve the areas that are lacking. If you are struggling with worries, anxiety, and stress, hold a Red Jasper in meditation and visualize it strengthening you so that you can be an immovable pillar no matter what life throws at you.

Garnet symbolizes commitment and passionate love, and can also be worn as an amulet of protection from dark and low vibrations. Fall symbolizes decay, decline, and even death, so stay strong emotionally and mentally with the help of Garnet. Protect your energy by balancing your Root Chakra and staying grounded. Wear Garnet daily to remind yourself that you are enough, you are worthy, and you are divinely protected.

Watermelon Tourmaline brings emotional balance and healing. It is said that during the fall, the veils between realms are thinner, meaning you can connect with your ancestors and passed loved ones a lot more clearly. This can bring comfort and happiness, but also grief and sadness. Watermelon Tourmaline comforts your heart and protects your emotions so that you can feel positive and hopeful.

Black Tourmaline

Clear Quartz

Green Calcite

Crystals for Winter

In winter the days are short and dark. During this time, it is important to take note of your dark side. Strive to evolve as you prepare for brighter days ahead and use the following Crystals during this sacred time of reflection and rest.

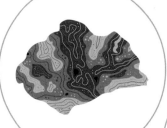

Cinnabar

Selenite

Angelite

Black Tourmaline is a Crystal of protection. It eliminates negative energy in any space, including your personal space. By holding it, wearing it, and meditating with it, you can create a shield of protection around you so that nothing gets near you without your permission. It also helps with the feelings of loneliness and depression common in the winter months.

Clear Quartz can help the winter blues. When you feel like you can't focus or that your mind is filled with negative thoughts, take a piece of Clear Quartz, hold it to your Third Eye Chakra, and pour all of your negative thoughts into the Crystal. You will feel so much lighter when you are done. Make sure to cleanse your Clear Quartz before its next use.

Green Calcite is here to aid you through feelings of sadness, anxiety, and stress that can be associated with winter. Its light green shades help to balance your Heart Chakra, giving a sense of renewed purpose and a desire to make positive changes in your life. It also encourages you to let go, forgive, and have compassion so that you can look past old memories and make new ones. Wear Green Calcite near your heart for comfort and emotional balance.

Angelite is your reminder that while winter can be a difficult time for many, you don't have to go it alone. There is always someone you can call on for help or lean on for support in the physical and spiritual realms. Angelite balances your Throat Chakra, facilitating your communication with others, giving you the confidence to speak your truth. Decorate your home with Angelite to facilitate communication with those you live with and those watching over you in the spiritual realms.

Selenite is a powerful energetic cleanser and light beacon. Not only can it help eliminate negative energy around you, but it can also prevent negative thoughts and emotions. Once it has cleansed negative energy it will bring bright light to illuminate your space and keep the vibration high. Place Selenite around your home in entrances, windows, and in the center of rooms so that it removes negative energy from your space.

Cinnabar is a Crystal of transformation because it takes you on a quest of self-discovery. Winter is a time to look within yourself for the truth and you can use it to check on yourself. How is this season making you feel? How do you feel about your relationships or job? Allow yourself to feel, think, and accept the truth. Then before you enter a new season, allow yourself to make the necessary changes. Cinnabar will bring opportunities since it is a prosperity and abundance Crystal. Gaze into your Cinnabar and journal about any immediate words or feelings it evokes; question what it is trying to tell you.

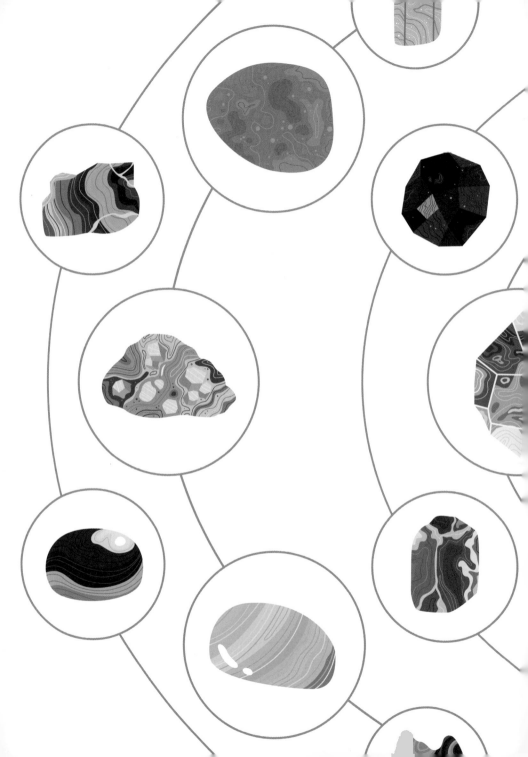

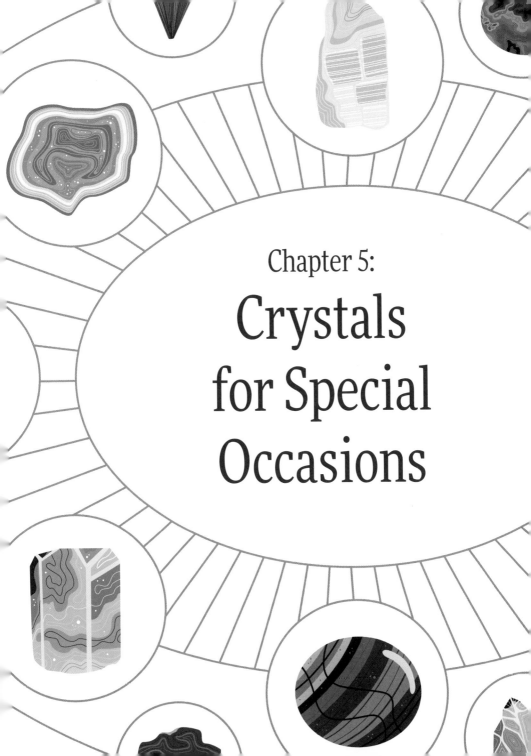

Chapter 5:
Crystals for Special Occasions

Fluorite

Amethyst

Lapis Lazuli

Crystals for Birthdays

Birthdays are the perfect time to shine bright, wear your best outfit, and make a big birthday wish. So blow out your candles and grab your favorite birthday Crystals from the list below. These Crystals are also great birthday gift ideas.

Sunstone

Citrine

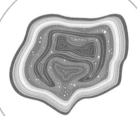

Blue Chalcedony

Amethyst is the perfect celebration Crystal. The Ancient Greeks believed that if you carried a piece of Amethyst with you, you could drink all day and night and never get drunk—its name comes from the Greek word *amethystos*, meaning "not drunk." Amethyst is a great birthday gift because it brings peace, tranquility, clarity of mind, and the ability to make good decisions. It also promotes rest and rejuvenates your body so that you can continue to have good health and many birthdays ahead.

Fluorite gives a sense of direction. Birthdays are a good time to look back on what you have accomplished in the past year, and to look forward to where you want to go in the next one. It is also a mind clearer that allows you to see your true attributes. Fluorite brings out the best in you so that you can recognize all that you have accomplished and will accomplish. Set new intentions into a Fluorite bracelet for your new year of life. Wear this bracelet to remind you of what you want to accomplish, and stay focused.

Lapis Lazuli gives confidence and increases self-esteem, and the Pyrite in this Crystal brings joy and energy in addition to attracting prosperity and abundance. On your birthday you deserve nothing but the best, so adorn yourself with a piece of Lapis Lazuli jewelry to stand out. Gifting this Crystal to someone on their birthday will make them feel like royalty.

Blue Chalcedony gifted as a birthday present will provide the recipient with harmony and clarity. Blue Chalcedony's energy is like that of a parent holding their child on their shoulders in a crowded area; it clears the way so that you can see your life from a true, honest, and realistic position.

Citrine is the embodiment of birthday well wishes. It is a Crystal of happiness, joy, and wealth, and brings a lively energy that keeps you mentally and emotionally healthy. It also attracts abundance and prosperity, teaching you that money is not the root of all evil and that in the right hands it can help many people. Citrine also reminds you that you are deserving of every great thing. Add a small Citrine to any birthday card to give the best of gifts.

Sunstone illuminates your path ahead and protects you from dark forces so that you may live a long and prosperous life. Have you ever heard someone say: "Happy solar return" on your birthday? This is referring to the Sun returning to the position in the sky it was in when you were born. For your new solar return use Sunstone for happiness, self-confidence, good luck, and success. Wear Sunstone as your birthday jewelry to ensure you have the most special day!

Blue Tiger's Eye

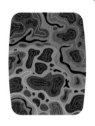

Brecciated Jasper

Chrysoprase

Crystals for a New Job or Promotion

New jobs are exciting, and you want to make sure you make a good first impression. You also want to make sure that the good impression continues so that it will eventually lead to a promotion. Use these Crystals to succeed at work.

Pyrite

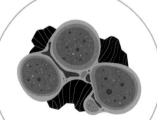

Prehnite with Epidote

Honey Calcite

Blue Tiger's Eye possesses good luck qualities and is especially powerful when it comes to new opportunities. It teaches that if you put your mind and intention into something you want, you will succeed every time. Blue Tiger's Eye helps stop negative self-talk and redirects those thoughts to be positive and uplifting. Keeping Blue Tiger's Eye with you at all times will help you thrive at any new job. It will also help you stand out in any evaluation for a promotion.

Brecciated Jasper brings out the leader in you and helps you encourage others so that your team runs like a well-oiled machine. You will find yourself taking care of the least desirable tasks with a good attitude, and this will help you stand out and be an asset to any team. Bring Brecciated Jasper to work with you daily.

Chrysoprase is a magical Crystal. Alexander the Great is said to have worn a piece on his belt, making him invisible and invincible in battle. It is perfect for keeping calm and not getting frustrated during stressful situations. It is also a Crystal for heart healing and it teaches you to love yourself and not fall back into unhealthy patterns. This ensures you develop healthy work relationships with good boundaries so that you stay happy and productive. Keep a piece of Chrysoprase in your workspace to develop happy, healthy work relationships (this may not happen immediately, but be patient while this Crystal works its magic).

Honey Calcite is a great Crystal for overcoming obstacles and building courage. If you feel there has been an injustice or something needs to be changed, Honey Calcite can help you harness the inner strength to stand up for what is right. It's also a great Crystal to help manifest the promotion you have been dreaming of. Write on a piece of paper exactly what that promotion looks like and spend a few minutes meditating on it with your Crystal.

Prehnite and Epidote are a power team that will help you endure any long-term stressful situations, as long as they are properly cleansed, charged, and programmed. Prehnite helps you declutter mentally and physically, clearing your mind of limiting thoughts, and allowing you to focus and concentrate. Epidote improves your capabilities and helps you keep up with the demands of any job. Place a Prehnite with Epidote at your workspace to emanate grounding and positive energy all around you.

Pyrite can help you live a joyful and fulfilling life. With Pyrite, you'll want to be your most authentic self and live a life of integrity because it brings you the strength to overcome struggles while also attracting abundance and prosperity. Everything you wish for you can receive with Pyrite energy. If a new job or promotion is what you desire, ask Pyrite to bring that to you and watch it work its magic!

Rainbow Moonstone

Pink Tourmaline

Hematite

Crystals for a Bridal Shower

At a bridal shower, the bride-to-be is showered with love by those closest to them. If you are a bride-to-be or planning a bridal shower for someone special, use the Crystals in this section to help you make it a memorable event.

Golden Topaz

Mangano Calcite

Kunzite

Rainbow Moonstone embodies feminine energy and can help you feel tranquil and serene in the most stressful times. Bridal showers are about uplifting the bride-to-be and Rainbow Moonstones encourage positivity from the sincerest place within your heart. Wear Rainbow Moonstone to feel sincere joy and heartfelt happiness, whether you are the party planner or bride-to-be.

Pink Tourmaline brings unconditional love, loyalty, and respect to a bridal shower. It brings out the best in you as the host or planner because it promotes friendliness. Pink Tourmaline is one of the best choices for jewelry for a bride-to-be, since it reminds you that you are worthy of receiving love and that if you have been hurt in the past, you can heal and open up again.

Hematite is a Crystal that can help ground energies and ensure you thrive no matter how stressful things get. If there are disagreements or confusion, Hematite quickly smooths things over so that you can communicate and make amends. Make goodie bags for the planning committee and include a small piece of Hematite.

Kunzite is a magical Crystal. If you've ever held a Kunzite, you will agree that it has a soft, love-filled, hug-like energy. It is your cheerleader as you practice heart healing. In friendship, it reminds you that when one of you thrives, you all thrive. Wear your Kunzite, get gushy, feel proud, and be there to support the bride-to-be on their special day.

Mangano Calcite has the perfect energy to help you celebrate and let go. The days leading up to a bridal shower might have been busy and packed with stress, but the day is here! Be happy, be merry, and enjoy yourself by letting go of all expectation and demands. Wear Mangano Calcite earrings so this energy can be activated and flow around your entire aura.

Golden Topaz is the perfect Crystal to use during the planning process of bridal showers because it boosts confidence and generosity, and decreases anxiety. If you are a bride looking to choose your wedding party, sit in meditation with this Crystal. It has the ability to bring helpful friends to your aid. If you are in charge of planning a bridal shower, carry this Crystal with you to spark the best ideas.

Peach Moonstone

Garnet

Rhodochrosite

Crystals for a Wedding

Weddings are a celebration of unconditional love and the ultimate party for many families. If you are attending a wedding and want gift ideas, are part of the wedding entourage, or are the one getting married, these are the Crystals for you.

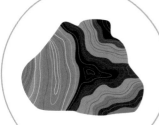

Emerald

Herkimer Diamond

Ruby Zoisite

Peach Moonstone is associated with the New Moon and new beginnings. It helps you understand and navigate your emotions, and allows you to be vulnerable and share feelings with the person you are closest to. Gift the happy couple Peach Moonstone to help them grow in their emotional intelligence and become closer than ever before.

Garnet may be the second wedding anniversary gemstone, but it's also the perfect gift for a wedding day because it represents reproduction, fertility, and wealth. Garnets bring passion and the strength to overcome any struggle, making them one of the best Crystals to gift any new couple about to take on the world together.

Rhodochrosite reminds you that self-love is where it all begins to have a healthy romantic relationship with another person. We must learn to love ourselves by performing acts of self-love and then we will know how we want to be loved. Once you can do that you will attract the right kind of love and not fall into the traps of an unhealthy relationship. Hold your Rhodochrosite and tell it how you want to be loved by your partner so that it can help make all of your love desires and intentions come true.

Ruby Zoisite is a combination of Ruby and Green Zoisite. Ruby represents passion and vitality, and Green Zoisite represents growth and fertility. When united, they bring joy, gratitude, and patience. If you are looking for a thoughtful wedding gift, a Ruby Zoisite sphere would be perfect since spheres represent balance, unity, and wholeness.

Herkimer Diamond packs a powerful punch since it absorbs positive energy from one end, and lets go of negative energy out of the other. Herkimer Diamonds are perfect to be worn by the bride as a necklace or by the groom as cufflinks. During the wedding day when everyone is sending the happy couple the best of wishes, Herkimer Diamonds can be used to bottle up this energy as a reminder of the happy day.

Emerald opens you up to giving and accepting love. If you have been hurt before and have put up barriers around your heart, Emerald will help you eliminate them. Emerald is a Crystal for successful love, the twentieth wedding anniversary gemstone, and a great gift for newlyweds to work with. Gift it to each other in special matching pieces, such as rings, bracelets or pendants, to connect you through the energy of Emerald.

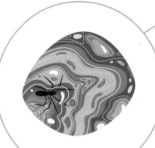

Amber

Black Tourmaline

Blue Lace Agate

Crystals for a New Baby

Starting a family is one of the biggest milestones in life. Having a baby can be scary and nerve-wracking, but so rewarding! If you are entering this new stage of life and would like a little comfort and guidance, use the following Crystals.

Malachite

Tiger's Eye

Green Apatite

Amber and its long, slow fossilizing process means it has gained wisdom from all it has endured. When you bring a new baby into your family, Amber guides you and helps you to believe in what you have to offer. It also puts you in touch with your higher self, where you hold all the answers. Combine Amber with other love-centered Crystals to make an amulet of love and protection. You've got this!

Black Tourmaline can create a shield of protection around you and your loved ones, especially a new baby. Many cultures believe in the evil eye, which is when a person can harm you or your baby by having envious thoughts toward you or them. For safety it's best not to put jewelry on babies but you can place a Black Tourmaline in their bedroom (out of their reach) or place one in your diaper bag, car, or stroller.

Blue Lace Agate is a Crystal of calm, patience, and communication. It can help you become so connected to your baby that you can understand what they are trying to tell you based on their cooing, cry, and what makes them laugh. This intuitive connection is so important. Place a Blue Lace Agate in your baby's bedroom (out of their reach) and ask the Crystal to create a strong telepathic bond between the two of you.

Green Apatite is a Crystal for healthy growth, physically, emotionally, and spiritually. Having a baby, especially your first, can be a daunting challenge. Green Apatite instills happy thoughts and prevents you from dwelling when you are struggling. It will give you a gentle kick so that you can move forward, making happy memories with your new family member. Keep this energy near your baby by making a cute Crystal craft such as a picture frame with Green Apatite chips and placing it in your baby's nursery.

Tiger's Eye reminds you of how lucky you are to have been chosen to have a baby, whether it is your first or your tenth. Tiger's Eye brings out the fun in situations and draws you closer to the people you love the most, enhancing and strengthening your family unit. Take some time when the baby is sleeping to start a gratitude journal. Meditate while holding a Tiger's Eye stone in your receiving hand and ask it to illuminate all of your blessings.

Malachite is known as the midwife stone because it assists any mother-to-be during the courageous act of childbirth and transformation. Malachite is a powerful heart healer, and it prepares any parent-to-be emotionally to love and be loved unconditionally. It also helps ground you so that you are not filled with worries and fears. Bring Malachite with you during the birth and you will have the most amazing companion during this time and post-partum.

Chrysocolla

Smoky Quartz

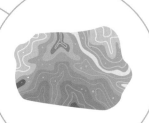

Rose Quartz

Crystals for Going on Dates

When you think about going on dates, you might get butterflies. But dates don't have to be scary; they can be fun. If you are single and ready to mingle, grab any of the following Crystals and open up to love.

Ruby

Morganite

Aquamarine

Chrysocolla balances your Throat and Heart Chakras and creates a connection between the two so that everything you say comes from a place of love. It helps you balance conversations by allowing others to speak and listen intently to what each party has to say. It also helps build your social skills, which will make you more comfortable and confident in social settings. The next time you go on a date take Chrysocolla with you so that conversation flows easily.

Smoky Quartz clears away unwanted negative energy that you are walking around with, such as energy from past relationships, so that you can attract better dates. It also stops negative patterns and old habits you might not even realize you have. Meditate with Smoky Quartz and visualize it cleansing and renewing all of the energy in your field.

Rose Quartz teaches you to love yourself first so that you can set the standard for the type of love you would like to receive from a romantic partner. Perhaps you think the kind of love you want doesn't exist, or that it's impossible for someone to possess all of the qualities you are looking for. This is where Rose Quartz comes in. It reminds you that you can manifest any partner you'd like because you control your destiny. See Chapter 7 to learn how to make a powerful manifesting grid.

Aquamarine is great for going on dates and will help communication flow like a peaceful river. It also helps you let go of judgments and preconceived notions about people, allowing you to find love where you might not expect it. Aquamarine lore states that couples used to wear this Crystal to build true love rather than a relationship based on lust. Wear an Aquamarine pendant that sits near your throat on your next date so that communication is free and easy.

Morganite is a Crystal of the heart and helps to heal from resentment, anger, and pain you are holding in your Heart Chakra. Once it has brought emotional balance, it brings back your desire to be loved and opens you up to accepting compliments from others, increasing self-esteem. Morganite can help attract your soulmate and deepen your current relationships. Wear Morganite daily if you are looking to get back into dating.

Ruby is perfect for people getting back into the dating scene because it helps you get your mojo back. There is nothing better than looking in the mirror and feeling good about yourself. It helps you tap into your sensuality, confidence, and self-power. Bring Ruby with you the next time you are out for a night of fun, or for your next hot date.

Iolite

Charoite

Danburite

Crystals for Graduation

Graduation is a well-deserved celebration for any student, marking the end of one chapter and the beginning of the next. The Crystals on this page celebrate graduations and offer support for future endeavors.

Black Kyanite

Black Moonstone

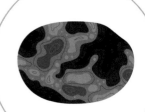

Rhodonite

Iolite is the perfect graduation Crystal because it is a navigator. By balancing your Third Eye Chakra, it helps you see clearly, tap into your intuition, and release obstacles in your way—this reveals the path you should take. It also helps you see what you need to work on to accomplish your highest achievement. Gift a graduate an Iolite to help them get to where they want to go.

Charoite helps you shed your old self, making way for who you are about to become. It is a stone of transformation and transition into the next chapter of your life. It supports big changes and removes any blockages in the way of progress. This might feel difficult at first, but Charoite's energy is there to support you through the process. Gift Charoite to a graduate for its positive transformation qualities.

Danburite is excellent for graduates who will be taking a break to do self-realization work, or travel. It is a Crystal of self-discovery and helps you connect with your Crown Chakra so that you can explore spirituality. Danburite facilitates your connection with angelic realms so that you know you are divinely guided and protected. Gift Danburite to a graduate who is on the way to learning more about themselves.

Rhodonite energy is like a tight hug from the universe. It reminds you to be proud of yourself, and that the greatest love is self-love. Rhodonite helps you to see yourself clearly and with compassion so that you may forgive and not be too tough on yourself. Give Rhodonite to a graduate to tell them they are loved and supported, and to remind them just how worthy they are.

Black Moonstone possesses the strength of the Moon. It encourages new beginnings and rebirth, making it perfect for the graduate who is nervous to start afresh. Black Moonstone helps you to tap into your emotions and reveal anything you are trying to push down, illuminating what you want and which path to take after graduation. Carry Black Moonstone daily to help you see the path more clearly.

Black Kyanite cleanses and grounds any anxiety, nervousness, and stress so that you feel loved and supported. Wear it under your graduation cap and gown to feel protected and grounded. If you need help tapping into your gifts and talents or finding your purpose, wear Black Kyanite to help you sort out your decisions for the future.

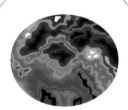

Moss Agate

Black Obsidian

Selenite

Crystals for a Housewarming Party

A housewarming party is common following a move, and gift giving is encouraged to help furnish a new home. The following Crystals are great gift ideas for new residents or even to use on the day of the party for setting the right mood.

Amethyst

Hematite

Ametrine

Moss Agate is known as "Gardener's Stone" because it not only brings grounding energies to your new home, but also keeps your garden and houseplants alive. This is also a drama-free Crystal that keeps attitudes and intense energies from rising in the home, fostering a nurturing, tranquil, and peaceful living space. Gift a piece of Moss Agate inside a new houseplant and both will encourage tranquility and emotional balance.

Black Obsidian is one of the most powerful Crystals for cleansing negative energy from a space. It acts as a shield of protection and absorbs negative energy. Place Black Obsidian at any of your home's entrances so that it can act as a filter and allow only good things to enter your space.

Selenite is one of the few Crystals that doesn't need cleansing and cleanses everything it comes into contact with. It clears your space of all negative energy and cleans other Crystals of the negative energy they have absorbed. Place Selenite in the bedroom to create a serene environment perfect for restful sleep, as its name comes from the Ancient Greek Moon goddess, Selene. You can also gift a Selenite tower lamp, which will light up any room and charge Crystal bracelets if you place them on top.

Ametrine is a rare Crystal that combines the qualities of both Amethyst and Citrine. Amethyst brings calm, peace, and harmony to any space, and Citrine brings joy, happiness, energy, abundance, and prosperity. Together, they bring clarity and relieve any tensions that might arise in a household, offering the perfect combination to create a harmonious and happy living environment. Gift Ametrine at any housewarming party to bring the new tenants peace, tranquility, abundance and happiness.

Hematite is a gentle, grounding, and protective Crystal. If you place a small tumbled piece of Hematite in each corner of every room of your home, you create a protection shield for your space. This shield will dissipate energy stuck inside and protect your home from any new negative energy entering. You can even place a piece of Hematite at every corner of the outside perimeter of your house, creating a protective energetic bubble for your home.

Amethyst embodies a peaceful, tranquil, and harmonious living space, creating a wonderful energetic foundation for a new home. If placed in the bedroom Amethyst will help you feel relaxed and can silence negative self-talk, anxieties, and worries so you can sleep. Amethyst is the ultimate gift for warming up any home.

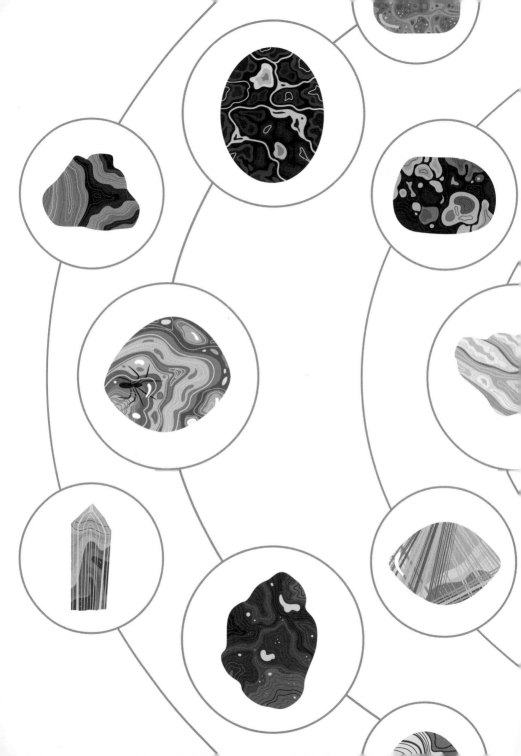

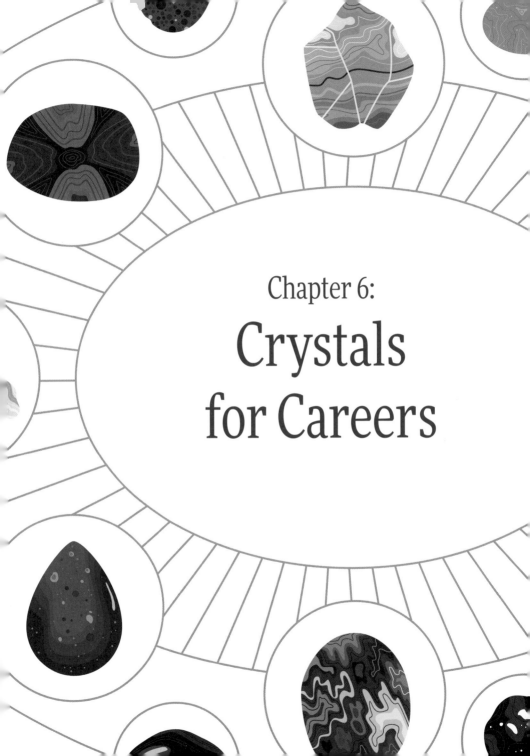

Chapter 6:
Crystals
for Careers

Blue Sapphire

Dumortierite

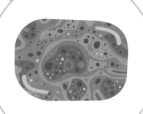

Green Aventurine

Crystals for Careers in Public Service

These Crystals can help improve and balance your mood, productivity, and focus. They are great for teachers, police officers, military, librarians, construction workers, politicians, lawyers and firefighters.

Amber

Hematite

Sodalite

Blue Sapphire brings forth a love for truth and integrity. In a career in which helping others is so important, it reminds you of why you decided to go into your field to begin with. It opens up your intuitive and psychic mind so you can use your wisdom and clearly and easily communicate with others. Invest in a piece of Blue Sapphire jewelry to wear daily while at work.

Dumortierite is the perfect Crystal for lifelong learners, and those in a career that is always evolving. It helps you to accept information presented to you with a clear mind, and helps you to see things from many different perspectives. Once you have made up your mind you will have the confidence to stand by your opinion and present it with emotional intelligence that others will respect. Keep Dumortierite near areas where you receive information, such as the office phone.

Green Aventurine is a happy-go-lucky stone with very sophisticated qualities. It encourages you to make new friends and gains you lifelong supporters that will be there for you through life's journeys. It's great for starting something new and following it through to the end, no matter how hard the road gets. It calls you to live a life in which you practice what you preach. Add it to your new office or workspace.

Sodalite encourages you to seek the truth and take fearless action. It also asks you to check in with your beliefs, taking off the blindfold and enabling you to make necessary changes if they are harming others. Sodalite also helps you detach and become lighthearted so that the opinions and judgments of others don't affect you negatively. Carry Sodalite with you if you are having a hard time being compassionate with others and yourself.

Hematite helps you stay grounded and keeps your thoughts organized and clear. By bringing mental clarity, Hematite helps you stay focused and in control of any situation. It's perfect for professionals who seek to bring justice and harmony to any disagreement or conflict. Hematite also helps you feel more confident and secure in yourself so that you don't let negative self-talk stop you from being successful in your field. Sit in meditation with Hematite and imagine it is directing roots from your spine into the earth so that you always feel rooted and grounded.

Amber encourages you to become an agent of positive change by helping you unlock your higher self to see how you can serve others. It gives you the energy and stamina to put in the daily work to make your unselfish dreams and ambitions a reality. Meditate with Amber and set your intentions around what you want to achieve in your career. Every time you start to lose heart, hold your Amber and let it remind you of your passion.

Shungite

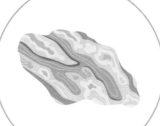
Pink Tourmaline

Kunzite

Crystals for Careers in Technology

Use these Crystals to improve and balance your energy, projects, opportunities, and confidence, particularly if you are a software developer, game creator, marketing professional, web designer, web developer, influencer, data scientist, IT manager, or in market research.

Picture Jasper

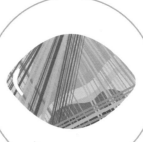
Rutilated Quartz

Emerald

Shungite helps block electromagnetic frequencies given off by electronics such as phones, computers, and microwaves. Energetically, Shungite will purify and eliminate any negative energies in your environment, clearing stress from the workplace. It is also very grounding so that you can focus on the tasks at hand. Place a Shungite in your workplace to create a more peaceful atmosphere.

Pink Tourmaline is the perfect Crystal for independent contractors. It helps you fall in love with your projects and be courageous enough to take risks since it helps you feel brave, independent, passionate, and empowered. It attracts new business relationships and clients as well as stimulating existing ones to bring you more opportunities. Bring Pink Tourmaline to business meetings to help you land the project.

Kunzite helps you to take pride in your work and to take on new projects with confidence, humility, and balance. It reminds you to be true to yourself and celebrate your uniqueness, and helps you be more tolerant of others. Kunzite assists in setting healthy boundaries between your personal and professional life, and helps you take constructive criticism with an open mind and heart. Carry Kunzite when meeting with potential new partners.

Emerald is a great Crystal for learning and retaining new information. It cultivates your intelligence so that you can continue to grow and make good choices when working with technology. It helps you overcome obstacles, setbacks, and misfortunes while remaining hopeful that things will improve. Wear Emerald when you have a difficult project to complete.

Rutilated Quartz awakens your creativity and stops you from procrastinating. It brings mental balance and stability and helps you enjoy life even when working. It also helps sharpen memory. Spend a little time meditating with Rutilated Quartz and setting intentions about how you want to grow professionally, doing what you love.

Picture Jasper eliminates any fears and insecurities you may have so that you have the confidence to pitch your ideas or take the initiative to start something new. People working in technology can be making new technological advances every day. Picture Jasper helps you see the bigger picture in projects you are working on and helps ensure your thinking is grounded so that you can tackle any difficult issues. Use Picture Jasper when working on group projects.

Green Calcite

Angelite

Lepidolite

Crystals for Careers in Wellness

These Crystals focus on healing, career advancement, and help balance energies in highly stressful positions. They are perfect for all medical professionals, including physical trainers, nutritionists, yoga teachers, Reiki healers, Crystal healers, home health professionals, physician assistants, and veterinarians.

Jet

Labradorite

Apache Tears

Green Calcite is a beautiful Heart Chakra Crystal that brings healing to healers. People in wellness give all of themselves to help others find healing and health, sometimes depleting their own batteries without recharging as often as they should. Green Calcite helps you live a life of dignity, love, and goodwill, promoting great compassion for all who are hurting, including yourself. Green Calcite also reminds you of your life's purpose so that you stay aligned with it. In stressful situations hold your Green Calcite, close your eyes, and take a few deep breaths. Visualize its soft green light creating a shield of protection and calm to soothe and ground you.

Angelite reminds you why you set out in this field, and inspires compassion. It also prevents work becoming routine. It helps you to continue giving your best so that you may bring healing to your community and yourself. Angelite is a high vibrational Crystal that promotes emotional intelligence, peace, and tranquility. Place Angelite where you see clients, to ensure it feels like a safe, healing space.

Lepidolite helps you manage stress. It reminds you that you come first and you need to make time for self-care, relaxation, and tranquility. Spending time laughing with loved ones can be perfect for inner healing and letting go of everything you've been hanging on to, bringing forth the amazing healer you are meant to be. Wear Lepidolite daily as a bracelet to protect yourself from lower vibrations entering your energy field, and to prevent you from picking up negative energies while working.

Apache Tears are the best Crystals for grieving and processing emotions. Sometimes we can be quick to bury emotions, but Apache Tears encourage you to sit with your feelings, process them, and to release them when you are ready. This will help you develop your emotional intelligence, which you can then use to help others process their emotions and grief. Carry Apache Tears with you in your pocket to bring positivity and lightheartedness.

Labradorite helps you get in touch with your psychic abilities so that you are more intuitive, aware, and led by your higher self. It gives you the confidence to trust in your gut feelings and helps you make decisions, even if others question them. Wear Labradorite where it can be admired by others, and share some of your magic with them.

Jet protects against negative energies that can bring down your vibration. It eliminates work-related stress that is fogging your mind, and it helps keep you calm and balanced. Jet reminds you to take care of yourself and to take the necessary time off to recharge and revitalize. Put Jet in your office or anywhere you spend the most time working.

Bronzite

Lapis Lazuli

Turquoise

Crystals for Careers in Customer Service

These Crystals assist with stressful situations, balance emotions, and encourage patience. They are great for retail and restaurant workers, sales, telecommunications, and hospitality professionals, flight attendants, drivers, chefs, health administrators, and logisticians.

Lava Stone

Hiddenite

Chiastolite

Bronzite is a soothing Crystal that encourages you to be gracious, courteous, thoughtful, diplomatic, and helpful to customers. It also helps you step out of your own emotions and be able to put others at ease. However, once you have clocked out, Bronzite also reminds you to be courteous and thoughtful with yourself. Place Bronzite in your sacred space to help ground and disconnect you from the outside world. Take the time to schedule time for yourself—you deserve it.

Lapis Lazuli wards off negative energy and only keeps the most positive of energies around. It helps you communicate from a place of integrity, kindness, and wisdom. Carry or wear Lapis Lazuli for protection, especially if you work with cash registers or expensive merchandise.

Turquoise supports you energetically and encourages you to keep learning to master your trade or product. It also helps you with your communication and delivery so that you can express your truth with confidence and poise. Turquoise possesses a great balance between masculine and feminine energy, helping you be both assertive and nurturing. Wear Turquoise jewelry to feel more confident on the job.

Chiastolite has wonderful properties that can help you tap into humility and patience. It also gives you confidence and helps you feel grounded when you are nervous or doubtful about a task. Chiastolite reminds you that you can accomplish anything you put your mind to. It also activates your creativity and practicality so that when you are presented with a hard task or customer,

you can think outside the box to come up with the best solution. Set an intention into your Chiastolite and place it at your altar so that it continues to guide you toward success.

Hiddenite is a green Heart Chakra Crystal that carries the most loving energies and brings healing and balance to the heart. It encourages you to be truly kind and helpful to others without expecting to gain anything, and will bring good karma and endless amounts of blessings. Hiddenite also helps to keep you calm, grounded, and clear-headed in the most stressful of situations. Take a deep breath and visualize the soft green light from Hiddenite creating a cloak of protection around you as you deal with high stress and anxiety. As you breath out, visualize your body letting go of the stress, allowing you to release all of the tension from your body.

Lava Stone brings you grounding because it has lots of Earth energy, and helps you communicate with others from a place of calm and cool collection. This can prevent anger, frustration, and anxiety even in times of high stress. Lava Stone fills you with clarity so that you can give the best service. Wear a Lava Stone bracelet and add a few drops of essential oil to the beads. Use Lavender essential oil for stress relief, Orange for bringing energy and awareness, and Rosemary for protection. The stone will absorb the oil and your bracelet will smell amazing all day!

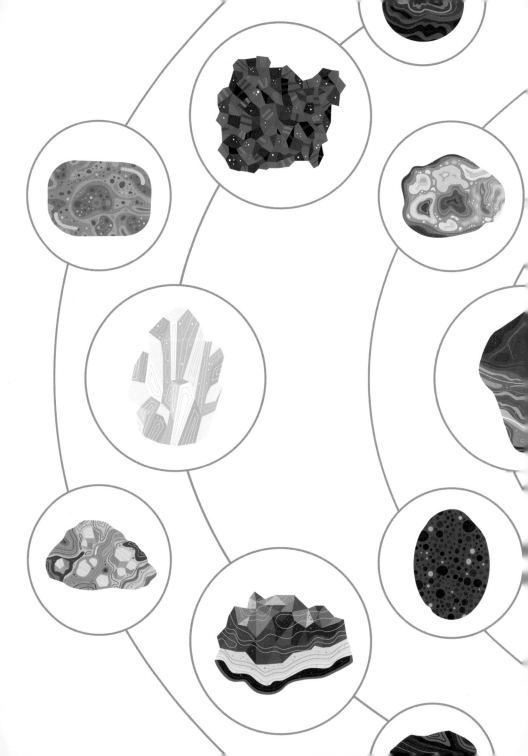

Chapter 7:

Practical
Crystal Grids

Crystal grids are shapes made up of Crystals working
together as a symphony or community, with the
collective goal of helping you achieve, heal, or
manifest a specific request. There is no right or
wrong way to do them; just let your intuition guide
you and make sure to have a clear intention.

Restful Sleep Crystal Grid

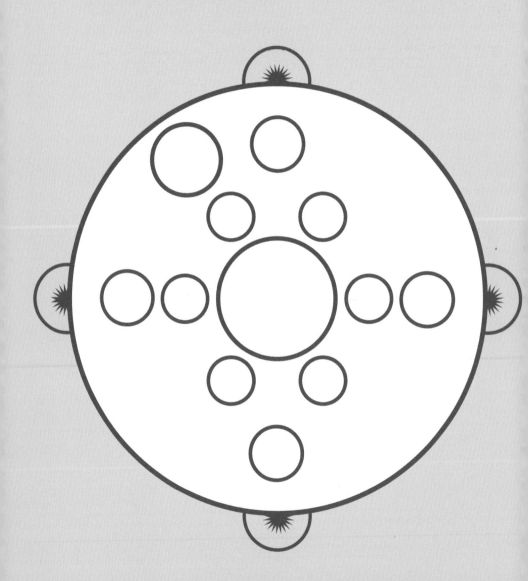

This grid will help improve your sleeping patterns. You will be working with Amethyst, the most popular better-sleep Crystal, Clear Quartz, the "Master Healer" and amplifier, and your intuition. You can use this example to create your own intuition-based Crystal grids.

You will need:

- A piece of paper and a pen
- 1 Amethyst point
- 6 Amethyst tumbled stones, clusters, or rough pieces. You can use a mix.
- 4 small Clear Quartz points
- 1 large Clear Quartz point

1. Find a sacred space to set your grid, such as under your bed where it won't be disturbed, or in a clutter-free zone away from pets or children.

2. Set an intention for your grid. What do you want to achieve, heal, or change? Write your intention on a piece of paper, fold it, then set it aside.

3. Cleanse your space and Crystals (see pages 7–8 for how to do this).

4. Place your grid generator (the Amethyst point) at the center of the grid with your piece of paper underneath it. (You can use the template opposite for guidance.)

5. Place the tumbled Amethyst stones around your Amethyst point.

6. Place your small Clear Quartz points around the edge of the grid symmetrically, or use your intuition to set them in whichever way feels right to you.

7. Take a few minutes to meditate on the intention of your grid and create an affirmation that summarizes what you want to manifest with it. For example: "Sleeping is a natural state for me. I will enjoy a full night's sleep and wake up recharged and rested."

8. Activate your grid by pointing your large Clear Quartz point to the Amethyst at the center of your grid (placing it in the final free circle in the template opposite). Visualize a line of light connecting the Crystals as you move the Clear Quartz point clockwise. As you do this, repeat your affirmation to yourself. Once you have completed the circle, your grid will be activated. You can also use your finger to activate your grid.

9. Leave your grid up for as long as you'd like, making sure to revisit it every so often to reactivate it if it's feeling dull.

10. When you're ready to deactivate your grid, remove the Crystals in the reverse order that you assembled them, from the small Clear Quartz points first, to the Amethyst point last.

Clear Quartz Full Moon Manifesting Grid

For this grid you will be working with Full Moon energy, the Sacred Geometry symbol the Flower of Life, and Clear Quartz. Clear Quartz is the "Master Healer" and can also be programmed to help you with any request. This grid is perfect for manifesting anything your heart desires. No intention is too big or too small, so don't be shy. Using this grid will also charge the Crystals with the power of the Full Moon, which you can use for other rituals.

You will need:
- A piece of paper and a pen
- A Flower of Life symbol (see opposite page)
- 12 small Clear Quartz points
- 6 Clear Quartz tumbled stones
- 2 large Clear Quartz points, or 1 large Clear Quartz and 1 Selenite wand with a point

1. Begin by setting up your scared space. For best results, create this grid on a flat surface that can be moved and placed under the Full Moon outside.

2. Cleanse your chosen space and Crystals (see pages 7–8).

3. Sit in meditation for a few minutes and journal about your intention for this grid. Write this on a piece of paper, fold it, then set it aside.

4. Place a large Clear Quartz point at the center of the grid, tucking your intention paper underneath. Place the tumbled Clear Quartz stones in the center of every flower surrounding the center. Finally, place the small Clear Quartz points in the center of each outer flower, facing the points outward so that the grid will send the energy out into the universe.

5. Create some affirmations that you can repeat to yourself when activating your grid, such as: "I am abundant. I am grateful for money. Money flows freely to me," or: "I am surrounded by love. My heart is open. Love is always flowing my way."

6. Activate your grid by pointing your large Clear Quartz point or Selenite wand to the Clear Quartz at the center of your grid, and visualize a line of light connecting the Crystals as you move the Clear Quartz point or Selenite wand clockwise. As you do this, repeat your affirmation to yourself. Once you have completed the circle, your grid will be activated. You can also use your finger to activate your grid.

7. Place your grid under the Full Moon overnight and bring it in before the Sun rises for best results. Place it somewhere it will not be disturbed so the power won't be deactivated. Leave your grid up for as long as you'd like.

8. When you're ready to deactivate your grid, remove the Crystals in the reverse order that you assembled them, removing the twelve Clear Quartz points first, and the large Clear Quartz point last.

Citrine, Pyrite, and Green Aventurine Spiral Grid

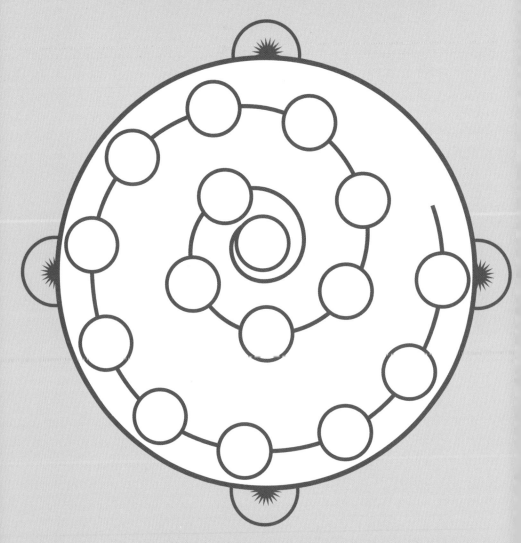

I don't recommend using more than four types of Crystals per grid because you want the energy to be focused and too many Crystals might create energetic confusion.

If you are looking for an easy way to increase your prosperity and abundance, this grid is the perfect ritual since it combines three wealth, opportunity, and prosperity Crystals: Citrine, Pyrite, and Green Aventurine. In this grid you will be using the spiral, a shape known for drawing in and radiating energy.

You will need:
- A piece of paper and a pen
- A spiral printout (see opposite page)
- 1 Citrine point or cluster
- 4–6 Green Aventurine tumbled stones
- 4–6 Pyrite tumbled stones or small rough pieces
- 4–6 Citrine tumbled stones
- 1 Clear Quartz point

1. Find a sacred space to set your grid where it won't be disturbed.

2. Meditate on your intention for this grid. What do you want to draw in? What types of abundance are you looking for? Write this on a piece of paper, fold it, set it aside.

3. Cleanse your space and Crystals (see pages 7–8), then take your Citrine point or cluster and hold it at your heart center. Close your eyes, take a deep breath, and send your intentions into the Crystal so that it knows what to do once activated. Repeat this step with your tumbled Green Aventurine, Pyrite, and Citrine stones.

4. Place the Citrine point or cluster on your grid at the center of the spiral, tucking your intention paper underneath it.

Next, place a tumbled Green Aventurine stone further along the line of the spiral, followed by a tumbled Pyrite stone, then a tumbled Citrine stone. Continue this alternating pattern until you have placed all your tumbled Crystals on the grid.

5. Create an affirmation that you can repeat to yourself when activating your grid, such as: "I attract money to me easily and effortlessly," or: "I draw opportunities, abundance, and prosperity into my life."

6. Activate your grid by pointing your Clear Quartz point at the Citrine point or cluster at the center of your spiral grid. Visualize a line of light connecting the Crystals as you move the Clear Quartz point along until the end of the spiral. As you do this, repeat your affirmation to yourself. Once you have completed the circle, your grid will be activated. You can also use your finger to activate your grid.

7. Leave your grid up for as long as you'd like or until you feel your intentions have been manifested. To cleanse, reactivate, or send the grid extra energy, repeat step six using your Clear Quartz point.

8. When you're ready to deactivate your grid, remove the Crystals in the reverse order that you assembled them, removing the tumbled Citrine, Pyrite, and Green Aventurine stones first, and the Citrine point or cluster last. You can also burn your paper with your intentions and bury the ashes in the ground.

Conclusion

Nine years ago when I brought my first Crystal home, I never thought I would be embarking on this Crystal healing journey, or imagined that I would one day write a book about Crystals. Life is filled with fun twists and turns. There is not one corner of my home that I don't have a Crystal in and I am so grateful to be working with these amazing Crystal allies. I leave you with three key pieces of practical advice for working with Crystals:

1. Remember that following your inner compass is crucial. When choosing a Crystal, no matter what their properties are on paper, follow your intuition. If you need help with self-confidence but a Crystal for prosperity is calling you, go with that one.

2. Don't forget to spend at least five minutes cleansing new Crystals and programming your intentions into them. This will make a world of difference when working with Crystals.

3. Have fun! Working with Crystals is so enjoyable. You have so many choices of color, texture, and energies. The possibilities are endless when it comes to picking your team of Crystals, so have fun with it!

I truly hope you have enjoyed reading this book and that it has brought you closer to the Crystals you connect with the most. I also hope you have learned a few ways to incorporate Crystals into your everyday life, and added some practical gems of information (no pun intended) to your toolbelt of healing knowledge.

Recommended Reading

People always ask me how I learned so much about Crystals. My answer is that it took me some time and that I naturally began to retain information on each Crystal because it's something I love. I am also a researcher and read up on anything I have questions about. Here are some Crystal books in my collection that I could not live without:

First book I ever bought on Crystals:
- *Healing Crystals* by Cassandra Eason

Classic books with metaphysical properties:
- *Love is in the Earth: a Kaleidoscope of Crystals, Updated* by Melody
- *The Crystal Bible: a Definitive Guide to Crystals* by Judy Hall

If you love the science and history of Crystals:
- *Rocks, Minerals & Gems* by Sean Callery and Miranda Smith

Rituals with Crystals:
- *Gem Water* by Michael Gienger and Joachim Goebel
- *The Book of Crystal Spells* by Ember Grant

New favorite find:
- *Crystal Basics Pocket Encyclopedia* by Nicholas Pearson

Acknowledgments

This book is dedicated to my mother Doris who is my angel in heaven. At first I asked myself why I couldn't have found Crystals before she left us but later I realized she was the one who led me to them. Gracias Mama por ser siempre la voz que me guia, Te quiero mucho. (Thank you, mom, for always being the voice that guides me, I love you.)

This book is also dedicated to my husband Dennis. I could not have written it without him. He is my biggest supporter, business partner, co-parent, and most importantly my best friend. I thank my lucky stars for you every day! Thank you for always believing in me and motivating me to keep going. I love you!

To Noah, Milly, and Memphis, my kids. I know Mommy has to work a lot but it will all pay off one day, I promise. You three are my motivation, what keeps me going. I am so proud of the exceptional humans you already are and can't wait to see all that you will do. I love you to the Moon and back again and again...

A special thanks to my Instagram family. Thank you for supporting me on The Healing Gem page every single day and showing me that I can be myself. I am so grateful for the lifelong friendships I have created there and without you I would have never come across the opportunities I have today!

Finally, I want to thank Chloe Murphy, Katerina Menhennet, and Jennifer Barr from Leaping Hare Press for supporting me through this process and believing that I could finish this book. Thank you for believing in me and giving me the courage to keep going.

About the Author

Kathy Banegas is a first generation El Salvadoran American from Los Angeles, California. She currently lives in San Gabriel with her husband and three kids. Before starting her business in Crystals and Healing she was in healthcare administration. In 2014, she found herself going through an emotional and traumatic crisis in her personal life after losing her mother to breast cancer. In the search to heal from depression, anxiety, and insomnia she found Crystals, and by early 2015 she had become an avid collector and believer in the healing energy of Crystals.

In 2015 she created and founded The Healing Gem, after realizing that Crystals helped both her and her husband, a disabled combat veteran. She enrolled in countless Crystal Healing and different healing modalities classes and by the end of 2016 she had become a Crystal Healing Master Teacher, Reiki Master Teacher, Sound Healing Master Teacher, and had received certifications in other classes such as Plant Medicine and EFT. In 2017 she quit her job and began to pursue her true passion in Crystals and Healing full time. Since then, Kathy has dedicated every day to teaching and educating people of all walks of life about the importance of connecting with their own ability to heal and the magic and energetic power of Crystals.

About the Illustrator

Viki Lester of Forensics and Flowers is a digital artist from London. Her training in graphic design has led to her bold illustration style, inspired by magic, botanicals, gothic art, and bright colors.

Index

Leaping Hare Press

First published in 2023 by Leaping Hare Press,
an imprint of The Quarto Group.
One Triptych Place
London, SE1 9SH
United Kingdom
T (0)20 7700 6700
www.Quarto.com

Design by Nikki Ellis
Production Controller: Maeve Healy
Commissioned by Chloe Murphy
Edited by Katerina Menhennet

A catalogue record for this book is available
from the British Library.

ISBN 978-0-7112-8460-9
Ebook ISBN 978-0-7112-8462-3

10 9 8 7 6 5 4 3 2 1

Printed in China

The information in this book is for informational
purposes only and should not be treated as a
substitute for professional counselling, medical
advice, or any medication or other treatment
prescribed by a medical practitioner; always
consult a medical professional. There is the
possibility of allergic or other adverse reactions
from the use of any ingredients, essential oils,
or other items mentioned in this book. The
author and publisher make no representations
or warranties with respect to the accuracy,
completeness, or fitness for a particular purpose
of the contents of this book and exclude all
liability to the extent permitted by law for any
errors and omissions and for any injury, loss,
damage or expense suffered by anyone arising
out of the use, or misuse, of the information
in this book, or any failure to take professional
medical advice.